THE BEST OF
REMINISCE

121

179

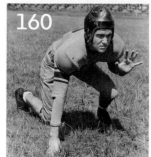

160

190

60

MEMORIES THAT LAST A LIFETIME

CONTENTS

PICTURED ON FRONT COVER:
Navy aviators on page 121, John Mahon
Marilyn Monroe on page 179, Pictorial Press Ltd/Alamy Stock Photo
Football player on page 160, DeWayne Owens
Mother and child on page 190, Kathy Gastellu
"Just married" car on page 60, Frederick Strassburger

PICTURED ON BACK COVER:
Flat tire pose on page 142, Elayne Dion
Father and son canoeing on page 44, Bruce Thompson
Fishing siblings on page 24, John Court
Marching band on page 148, Steve Gold
Pilot on page 88, Mark W. Johnson

©2018 RDA Enthusiast Brands, LLC.
1610 N. 2nd St., Suite 102, Milwaukee, WI 53212-3906

International Standard Book Number: 978-1-61765-758-0
Library of Congress Control Number: 2017963393
Component Number: 117300058H

Join the conversation at FACEBOOK.COM/REMINISCEMAGAZINE

103

67

124

199

86

4

156

Stories to Cherish

At *Reminisce*, we're all about remembering the past and bringing back the good times. Those sentiments are the heart and soul of this book, *The Best of Reminisce*.

Childhood meant lots of summertime escapades with friends, time spent obsessing over favorite bands, and tough (but important) lessons from Mom and Dad, which is exactly what you'll find captured in **Growing Up.** Family time is always a reason to celebrate, and that's why the picnics, parties and reunions in **All in the Family** feel so familiar. In the **True Love** chapter, you'll see how romance can (and often did!) appear when you least expect it—sometimes even through a rendezvous at the circus or between pen pals who became much more.

Paging through the book, you'll discover stories about rites of passage, such as joining the military (keep a tissue on hand—this section gets emotional) or finding a fabulous new job. Then put the pedal to the metal and cruise over to **Motoring Memories,** a chapter all about the cars that first made our hearts race. Other chapters reveal our passion for fun and games, fashion and fads, famous movie stars and sports icons.

Whether it was a boisterous uncle who accidentally cracked a Thanksgiving dish, a mom's detailed care in creating the perfect Halloween costumes, or a big family surprise at Christmas, the stories in **Happy Holidays** wrap things up with heartwarming reminders of simpler times.

Memories are precious bits of history. Let's keep sharing them.

The editors of *Reminisce* magazine

GROWING UP

Learning the ropes, creating long-lasting friendships and experiencing the thrill of new adventures were all part of the fun of being a kid.

CHAPTER 1

Short-Lived Winnings

*A young boy's memorable moment turns into a bonding experience
for him and his father many years later.*

JOHN J. ZILLIOX • WILLIAMSBURG, VA

A photographer behind the trumpet section snapped John's picture while
he led Sammy Kaye's big band in a Dixieland jazz tune.

Big Bands were all the rage in the 1940s. Most had a signature sound you could identify within the first few notes. Often, the bands performed between shows at movie theaters.

In November 1944, I decided to attend the Monday morning opener with Sammy Kaye's orchestra at Shea's Buffalo Theatre along with three friends from the South Park High School Orchestra. During his shows, Sammy would engage the crowd by calling out, "So you want to lead the band?" and every teenage musician responded, "You bet I do."

When that segment arrived, Sammy asked the question, we waved our hands, and he pointed to our group. The boys decided I should go on stage. I joined two other contestants—a young girl and a middle-aged man. We were interviewed and given souvenir batons. Then we took turns leading the band in "Tiger Rag." I won the competition by audience applause.

But it didn't end there. Sammy Kaye performed for the rest of the week, and by Friday four finalists, including me, were chosen to appear that night. I attended that evening and came away with a $25 war bond. A sailor and a soldier had finished in first and second place. So when I got home and bragged to my family that I had finished in third while the country was at war, it felt like first place as far as I was concerned.

My brother, who went to the theater on Monday after school, added, "Holy mackerel! That was you leading the band in the picture in the lobby!"

My father looked at me and said, "Your picture was in the lobby Monday afternoon? It had to be taken that morning to be printed by the afternoon. You skipped school. Well, Mr. Band Leader, you will not profit from this truancy."

He reached across the table, plucked my baton and war bond, and left the room. Sammy Kaye was never mentioned in my presence again, until...

Years later I complained to my father about my son skipping school. A look of remembrance came across his face and he left midconversation. He came back about a half-hour later and handed me the baton and war bond.

"I'm sorry, son. I meant to return these a long time ago. If it's any consolation, when you cash the bond, it will have a lot of interest on it and be worth more than $25."

"Thanks, Dad," was all I could say. Receiving them from his hand was almost as exciting as receiving them 30 years earlier.

Sliding into the Past on a Flexible Flyer

Frozen rivers and makeshift sledding paths create a wild ride.

ANDY CZARNECKI ◆ WEARE, NH

When I was in the fourth grade, in 1952, I lived with my Aunt Mae in Milwaukee, Wisconsin. I certainly remember walking to school when it was 10 below with half a blizzard blowing.

Aunt Mae would put my long johns on the radiator in the dining room, and I'd shiver as I got dressed until the warm underwear was on—aah! Then a bowl of oatmeal, getting dressed in scumpty-ump layers till I looked like Charlie Brown, and off to school I'd go.

My boots—we called them galoshes or artiks—were black rubber with metal fingers that fit into a slotted loop, and they were ice cold. You depended on your two pairs of socks and your shoes to keep your feet warm.

After school I'd head for a city park on the Milwaukee River. Kids would usually sled along the sidewalk that sloped down to the riverbank, but the day that I brought my brand-new Flexible Flyer, I had my own idea. "Heck with that," I said to myself. "I'm going straight down the hill and shooting out on the river." (Back then, the river usually froze solid around Thanksgiving.) I picked a spot where, if I traveled in a straight line, I would intercept the sidewalk about halfway down the hill. Off I went.

Well, I hit that sidewalk at a good clip—and then I went airborne for about 25 feet, slammed down onto the snow, and zoomed out across the river almost to the other side. If I had seen someone else do it, I would not have tried it. But once I'd done it and realized I'd survived, I was OK. In fact, it felt awesome! After that, it became old hat.

If you didn't have your own sled, you could rent a toboggan for 25 cents. The city had a ramp from the river level and workers somehow froze water on it, top to bottom. They had another smooth ramp right next to it, and a set of stairs next to that. You hauled the toboggan up the smooth ramp as you climbed the stairs to the top. When you were ready, a park employee released the safety on the gate, and you were off down the ice chute. You were moving when you hit that river ice!

It was a long hike back across the river and up the ramp each time. As it got darker out, that whole section of river was lit up.

On the walk home, about 3 miles, I'd spend the whole time thinking of my aunt's good food. I wasn't tired, or sore, or cold. It was only later, after I got into bed, that I realized I'd had a workout.

And the next morning? Let's do it again!

> " *But once I'd done it and realized I'd survived, I was OK. In fact, it felt awesome! After that, it became old hat.* "

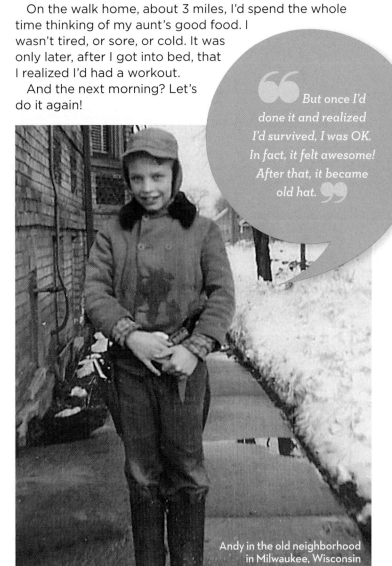

Andy in the old neighborhood in Milwaukee, Wisconsin

Best Sled for Snow Country

We lived in snow country, so my dad bought me a Lightning Guider sled in the 1940s. The factory where the sled was made was in Duncannon, Pennsylvania, about 30 miles from our home. My sister, Martha, my friends and I often went sledding in the snow or on the local ice-skating ponds and creeks. My own four children used this sled in the 1970s and '80s. I dragged the sled to Florida when my husband and I moved here in 1987.

NOVELLA WENDT LENGEL ◆ PALM BAY, FL

On an icy pond in Snyder County, Pennsylvania, Novella (below) ice-skates while pushing the wooden sled and her sister, Martha Wendt. That was 1954; today, Novella still owns her Lightning Guider.

Little House, Big Lessons

Laura Ingalls Wilder's pioneer life inspired generations of readers.

SARAH LAKE ◆ MEADVILLE, PA

A s a girl who loved the stories of Laura Ingalls Wilder, every night I would pull on a long cotton nightgown that I imagined Half-Pint (Pa's nickname for Laura) would have worn. Then my grandmother would tuck me into bed and read me a chapter from one of Laura's books. I'd imagine I was Laura, strong and brave, facing the cold prairie winters, listening to Pa's fiddle, riding in covered wagons or tending to the fields. Laura's stories became my stories; her memories became my memories.

I really enjoyed reading about how the Ingallses celebrated Christmas. Today, things are so fast-paced, it's nice to read about a time that was simple and easy. I'm reminded to keep it slow or you'll miss something.

Now I have five boys and a young daughter of my own, Rachel. It's my turn to tuck her into bed, sit in the reading chair and read aloud the same stories that sparked my imagination at her age. I watch her face light up when Laura exacts revenge on Nellie Oleson along the banks of Plum Creek. And I smile, because I know these stories are now her stories, too.

PORTRAIT: ROSE WILDER LANE COLLECTION, COURTESY OF HERBERT HOOVER PRESIDENTIAL LIBRARY; BOOKS: JONNY WHITE/ALAMY STOCK PHOTO

Kindness Rules

Jealousy transforms into a deep friendship after one simple gesture.

LUCILLE PEOPLES ◆ HENRYETTA, OK

Our friendship began in the summer of 1952. The first time I saw Carolyn, I was smitten with jealousy. She walked by my house wearing the prettiest dress, with shiny shoes to match. I stared at her with my meanest look.

The following week, she walked by again. This time I not only stared but I also stuck my tongue out at her. She looked a bit scared, but she waved and smiled. No, I did not smile back.

So it began. She seemed to wear a different dress every time she walked by. Once she even wore a hat, and it was pretty, too. I told myself it was ugly, just like her and all her fancy clothes.

Then one day my brothers and I went swimming at the city pool. We hadn't been there very long when I saw her and thought, *I just might really have to drown her.*

But I didn't. She came over and asked me if I was hungry. I thought of mean things to say but replied that yes, I was hungry. She told me her grandmother lived across the street and we could go there and get something to eat.

I had my doubts but soon found out her grandmother really did live across the street from the swimming pool. We went there and ate vanilla wafers and apples.

By the time we started the sixth grade together, we'd become inseparable. My friend Carolyn was awesome. She was always sharing, and she was so kind to me and to others.

The years passed. We married, had children, and now and then spent some time together. My mother passed away in 1961, and even though the church was full, the only person I saw as I walked down the aisle to leave was Carolyn, my best friend. She had driven to our old

Carolyn's smile helped turn Lucille into her best friend.

hometown to attend the services and be there for me.

I have so many memories of our friendship—some happy, some sad, but each one special. Thank you, Carolyn. You taught me that kindness rules over meanness and to care is to share.

ALL DRESSED UP FOR EASTER

SMILES AND NEW OUTFITS welcome the spring. Andrews sisters, from left, Colleen, 2, Kathleen, 4, and Maureen, 3, and brother Jim, 6, show off their mom's sewing skills in matching outfits in Coventry, Rhode Island, in 1962. "We dressed alike for all holidays," says Kathleen, now of Rochester Hills, Michigan.

Prom on a Boat

The class prom in 1970, my junior year at Moores Hill High School in Aurora, Indiana, was on a party boat. The Ohio River was nearby, and since the juniors hosted the dance, we opted to take a cruise. Prom goers met at school, and buses drove everyone to the ferry landing. The local paper took photos of me with my date, left, and a bevy of early arrivals, below.

SAM BENTLE ◆ AURORA, IN

> *We paid for the party boat with the money we made from our food stand at the annual Aurora Farmers Fair held every fall.*

HE'S GOT TWO HEADS

IMAGINE RUNNING into a two-headed ghost on Halloween night. Bill Herzog of Ann Arbor, Michigan, made the ghostly costume for his 11-year-old son, Don, out of a bedsheet and a mop named George. "Don held the mop handle," says Bill, "and was able to turn the mop head to face him when he talked."

> *While kids form a line, my daughter and her grade school classmate take a bite at apples swinging from the ceiling at a Halloween party in our rec room.*
>
> **MICHAEL LACIVITA**
> YOUNGSTOWN, OH

Majorettes on Parade

My sisters Sharon, Doris and Betty, along with our Aunt Sue and I, were in the American Legion's majorette unit and marched in every holiday parade in Toledo, Ohio, in the early 1950s. There were 12 kids in my family—seven sisters, five brothers—but we were the majorettes.

Our uniforms were royal blue corduroy with gold roping, and we wore wrist cuffs and hats that had inner cardboard liners. Our mother, Evelyn Clarke, and grandmother Gertrude Gross made the uniforms by hand.

Our favorite parade was on Memorial Day, when we marched to the cemetery along with several hundred friends and family watching and celebrating. When we arrived at the cemetery, priests said Mass in the open area and dedicated it to the fallen soldiers. At that time, even the kids knew the real meaning of Memorial Day and respected the ceremonies. After the ceremonies, it was time for picnics, fireworks and baseball at Joe E. Brown Park.

Remembrance, food, family and fun—there was no better way to celebrate Memorial Day than that.

HELEN PRICE ◆ SPRINGFIELD, IL

Break time for twirlers, from left, Aunt Sue, Sharon, Helen, Doris and Betty

IN THE MID-1960s, I was a seventh-grader at a rural Catholic school in northeast Wisconsin, looking forward to serving as altar boy at my first funeral Mass. Not only would I get out of school, I'd be invited to the bereaved family's home for dinner, complete with wonderful Bohemian desserts.

After Mass, we all walked over to the parish cemetery. The priest was giving a final blessing before the coffin, which was on a riser above the grave site, would be lowered into the ground. I stood between two other altar boys, holding a large cross that was considerably taller than me and felt as if it outweighed me by several pounds.

One of the boys asked if I knew how deep the grave was. Curiosity got the best of me. I stepped forward to check, but as luck would have it, there was loose gravel on top of the grass. Before I could catch myself, I slipped underneath the casket and into the grave. The cross wasn't spared; it came down with me.

As the other altar boys scrambled to help me, I saw the priest's cold stare. But others were smiling and giggling once I was safely on solid ground again.

That was the first and last funeral Mass I served at.

And in case anyone is wondering, the grave was 6 feet deep.

JAMES SCHIEGG ◆ OSHKOSH, WI

Thomas (right) with his first rock trio, a garage band inspired by the Fab Four. Dad was slightly impressed.

On the Rocky Road to Dad's Heart

I formed a rock band in the mid-1960s, and when we weren't practicing in our garage or the drummer's basement, we were listening to Beatles records, trying to figure out the chords and harmonies. We would watch Beatles movies, not for the plot (well, who did?), but to study their hands as they each played their instruments. For us, it was all about Beatles, Beatles and even more Beatles.

Dad seemed impressed that we could reproduce some of the songs, but his taste in music was pretty much limited to cowboy western—Gene Autry, Roy Rogers and the Sons of the Pioneers. He disliked rock 'n' roll and "those darned ol' Beatles" most of all.

That is, until he heard a song that struck his fancy, "Rocky Raccoon." When he found out it was a Beatles tune, he was surprised. Perhaps he thought the Fab Four had finally come to their musical senses. In any case, he liked Paul McCartney's nasal parody of an Old West saloon shoot-out over a woman—"Her name was Magill, and she called herself Lil/ But everyone knew her as Nancy."

Mom wanted to surprise Dad with a recording of "Rocky Raccoon" for his birthday, but it wasn't available as a single. She had to buy the album, *The Beatles*, commonly known as *The White Album*. The 30-song LP had several hard-rock tracks, including "Helter Skelter," "Birthday" and "Back in the U.S.S.R.," along with a couple of oddballs, such as "Everybody's Got Something to Hide Except Me and My Monkey" and "Why Don't We Do It in the Road?" Of course, Dad didn't care for any of them.

He liked just three songs, "Rocky Raccoon" and the old-timey "Martha, My Dear" and "Honey Pie." Unfortunately, Mom had bought the album on cassette, which made it difficult to locate the tracks Dad liked quickly. So she planned ahead. She kept "Rocky Raccoon" cued up for those times when Dad wanted to hear it without having to listen to any song he didn't like.

Who knows? Perhaps if Dad had lived in the era of programmable CDs, he might have become a rock-solid Beatles fan.

THOMAS JONES ◆ PICKFORD, MI

Highway to Seattle

Forget dirty deeds (done dirt cheap), all it took to see AC/DC was trust.

DOROTHY GAIL BROWN • CASA GRANDE, AZ

We lived on Orcas Island, Washington, an hour ferry ride plus a 1½-hour drive from Seattle. When our son Nick was 13, his favorite band was AC/DC. He was consumed with desire to see them in concert. His dad, Doug, and I assured him they would come in a few years.

"In a few years?!" Nick cried. "They won't last that long. They aren't that good. I hope they'll come sooner than that."

But wouldn't you know it, a short time later, on Feb. 12, 1982, AC/DC was scheduled to play a concert in Seattle, and one of Nick's friends had four tickets. The other boys were at least two or three years older than Nick, and as far as we knew, they would be without a chaperone. I offered to go, but the thought of having Mommy tag along didn't sit well with the group. So Doug and I said no.

Nick was heartbroken, and he resorted to begging. Still, the answer was no. Then I found a three-page letter from Nick expressing his fierce longing to go to the concert.

As the only fourth-grade teacher on the island, I was always concerned about what people would think. What would they say about my parenting skills if I succumbed to his pleas?

At 13, Nick was in despair about missing his favorite band—until his parents, Doug and Gail, relented in an act of love.

Although I have tried to change through the years, I have to admit that sometimes I feel my whole identity is based on what people think of the fourth-grade teacher!

I did what I always did: I invited my three best friends, all of whom had children around Nick's age, to talk it over with me. Colleen, Kathy and Marcia all agreed that Nick's going to a rock concert in the city was a bad idea. I shared their thoughts with my husband.

Doug is the kind of person who doesn't define himself by what others think. He read Nick's letter again and we discussed the situation for about an hour. Then we made our decision.

When Nick came upstairs the following morning, he looked downright despondent. I told him we had arrived at a verdict.

"We have decided you can go."

"Why?" Nick asked, surprised. "Was it something your friends said last night?"

"No," Doug replied. "It's because of the kind of son you've been for the past 13 years."

Nick's smile lit up the room.

As it turned out, Shane's mom went with the boys and they returned in one piece, none the worse for wear.

Many years later, Nick ended up taking his daughter Peyton to an AC/DC concert when she was 10 years old. Looks like the band was good enough to last, after all. AC/DC is still Peyton's favorite band.

Long live rock 'n' roll!

Holding on Through Shakes, Rattles and Rolls

We experienced the thrill of seeing many favorite musicians live. **JO MELE** ◆ MORAGA, CA

> " The music was truly American—loud, energetic and wild. It was new, and it was ours. "

The last card I opened on my 16th birthday in 1957 was from my boyfriend, Joe. It contained two tickets to Alan Freed's Rock 'n' Roll Show at the Paramount Theater in Brooklyn, New York.

At Flatbush and DeKalb avenues in Brooklyn, a huge line of teenagers wound around the block, waiting to buy tickets, while another, shorter line was for those with tickets. Joe and I felt a little overdressed standing there in the midst of the denim-and-bobby-sox throng. He had on a suit and tie, and I wore a black-and-white polka-dot dress, with crinolines, stockings and patent heels.

Inside, we climbed the four flights of stairs to the balcony and then made our way carefully down to our seats. Talk about nosebleed seats. With the pushing crowd, I pictured myself missing a step and landing flat on my face.

There were about 20 acts. Everyone who'd made a hit record that year seemed to be on the program. We saw the Platters, Buddy Holly and many other groups that night. The glitter from all the rhinestones and sequins on stage was dazzling. My favorite was Fats Domino, who belted out "Blueberry Hill" and "Ain't That a Shame." Fats must have soaked a dozen handkerchiefs during that performance.

Bill Haley and the Comets played "Shake, Rattle 'n' Roll" and "Rock Around the Clock." When the balding Haley slid down on his knees to play a solo, girls fainted.

The foot stomping shook the balcony. Kids danced in the aisles and sang along. No one stayed seated. The house went silent only while Chuck Berry played "Maybelline," and when he was done, near hysteria ensued. The girls pulled their hair as if possessed, and bawled. I held on to Joe. He seemed to be the only thing that wasn't shaking.

The music was truly American—loud, energetic and wild. It was new, and it was ours.

ALAN FREED was the first to adopt the term "rock 'n' roll" to describe the music he played on his radio show in the early '50s.

Pen Pals Stayed in Touch

Distance wasn't a factor for an adviser-turned-friend.

ARLENE R. METRIONE ◆ HACKETTSTOWN, NJ

Mildred Webinga Freeman was an English teacher at the new middle school I went to in the ninth grade. She wasn't my teacher; she was the adviser to the safety patrol on which I served. I loved being around her and enjoyed her sense of humor and kind personality. She was also a good listener.

At the end of the year, she announced that she was moving to Florida, and I was devastated. We exchanged addresses and became pen pals. I could tell her anything, and she treated me with respect even though I was a teenager.

In Florida, Mrs. Freeman became a Realtor, but she managed to find time to write letters, often while "sitting on" a model home awaiting customers. She wrote amusing stories and always took my concerns seriously.

She had given me an open invitation to visit, and I missed her so much. When I wrote to take her up on the offer, she answered, "Get your shoes on and your bags packed! You are welcome anytime!"

I spent three weeks with her in Miami, thrilled to do anything from washing dishes to touring houses with her. Her love of poetry, music and creative writing encouraged me to pursue these endeavors. One day while hanging sheets out on the clothesline, she looked up and said, "You know, the sky is fuel for the soul." I have never looked at the clouds since without hearing those special words.

Two years later, she surprised me by attending my high school graduation. Later that year, my family decided to spend Christmas in Florida and I couldn't wait to see my friend again. When I arrived at her house. I hoped to talk to her about school, but instead I found her in a hospital bed in the guest room. She had cancer of the liver, and family members were caring for her. I was in shock.

A month after we got back home, we received a call that Mrs. Freeman had died. To this day, more than 50 years later, I still see her smile and think about the advice she gave me. Now and then I reread her letters, and I remember the importance of her smile and her friendship.

Teacher and safety patrol adviser Mildred Freeman became Arlene's pen pal and lifelong friend.

Buzz cuts cued the start of summer for most boys in the early 1960s. Mark shows off his cut, above far right.

Counselor's Bluff

No one comes back from summer camp without a scary story or two to tell.

MARK STEFFEN • LEO, IN

The highlight of my summers in the 1960s was going to YMCA camp for a week. I was in elementary school in Richmond Heights, Ohio, and fundraisers helped to pay for the trip. I went door to door selling bars of soap or boxes of chocolate-covered mints. My parents always bought at least a carton of whatever I didn't sell.

While at the camp, we stayed in cabins, did craft projects, played ball, went swimming and sat around the campfire at night listening to the counselors tell scary stories. One night they told us not to leave our cabins after dark because there was a hermit living in a cave nearby who came out at night to kill his prey. Of course, that night we all slept with one eye open.

The next morning as we gathered to raise the flag, one of the campers yelled, "Look, there's blood around the base of the flagpole!" Pandemonium ensued until one skeptical camper took a closer look and informed us that the blood was merely berry juice. With that story put to rest, we all slept a lot better.

After swimming and working on craft projects, Mark made sure to write his folks about the candy bars at bedtime.

Hi Mom and Dad, We live in a cabin and we get a candy bar every night. And I go swimming every day. I'm going to make a wallet Monday and writing to you Sunday. *mark*

8-14-1960

August 7, 1961   Monday

Dear Mom,

My Counselor's name is Dave and my Junior counselor's name is Rick. I have a lot of nice cabinmates. At night we get a candy bar and whoever is the best in the cabin for the day gets an extra candy bar. As soon as the lights go off we'll here a story and lesson to the radio. My cabin is in a part of the woods called Gilon. I wrote this letter during rest period after lunch. Our cabin is going to have a game of softball with cabin 34 as soon as rest period is over.

Mark

P.S.

PLEASE SEND ME MY MONSTER Funny Books if You Can. Thanks

MY FATHER owned a grocery store in Logan, Ohio, in 1937. A Coca-Cola salesman called on him, saw me, and asked if he could take my picture for the company magazine. I was 5 and he told me I looked like Shirley Temple. I thought it was pretty cool.

ALICE J. HARVEY ◆ SCOTTSDALE, AZ

Let's Go Fly a Kid

A crazy idea creates a moment of flight.

THOMAS TURMAN ◆ BERKELEY, CA

My father's crazy airplane buddies, who hung out at the local airfield, gave me some unusual adventures when I was growing up in the 1940s.

One Saturday, Jerry, one of the craziest and my favorite of the test pilots, told of an idea he'd seen in a magazine. You take a large weather balloon, fill it with helium and cover it with a parachute. The parachute harness holds the pilot, who wears a belt with several weights. He controls the balloon's action by dropping weights to go up and by releasing gas through a valve on the filler tube to go down.

"It's called balloon jumping," Jerry said. "With the right balance, you can jump and glide over cars and buildings and such."

When Jerry mentioned that he had an old weather balloon and a parachute, the group decided to try it—with me.

"Yeah, he doesn't weigh very much," someone said.

They did a test run using a heavy toolbox strapped to a lawn chair.

Then it was my turn.

I strapped on the harness and the leaded belt as Jerry tied a knotted tether to me. I was so weighted down that I couldn't get the balloon away from the hangar. I started dropping the weights one at a time. Soon I felt a little lift. Then my feet came off the ground. I hit the helium valve and my feet once again grazed the lawn.

I dropped two more weights and rose so quickly that the tether line zipped through Jerry's hands. He managed to grab one of the line's knots as I floated about 20 feet in the air.

"It works!" Jerry cried. All the pilots were running along under me, laughing.

That was the best feeling ever. I didn't want to come down, but my dad was really shouting now, "Hit the valve! Hit the valve!"

I floated down very slowly until Jerry hauled on the line, dragging me down into the middle of the laughing men.

Having a Ball on the Concrete

In his Brooklyn, kids had fun the hard way. **BILL ABRAMS** ◆ PINE PLAINS, NY

Here I am in 1946, in all my glory, complete with cowboy hat and shorts (bottom right), in Brooklyn, New York, where I lived with my family in a cramped apartment.

Like kids everywhere, we found our fun outside, though our playground was concrete.

The brick wall behind me was the back of a theater that ran almost half a city block (about 100 feet). We used the long wall for games—handball, Chinese boxball (handball with an extra bounce) and a two-person version of stickball, which used a box drawn on the wall. If you threw the ball past the batter and it hit inside the box, it was a strike. The batter, who was facing forward, had to take the pitcher's word for it, and that could lead to a lot of, um, debate.

The apartment buildings had stoops with outdoor steps, where we played promotion, in which one kid was the teacher and the rest pupils. The teacher held a leaf in a clenched fist and had a pupil guess which hand had the leaf. Each pupil had a turn every round. If you guessed correctly, you advanced a step. Whoever reached the top first was the winner.

You could cheat for a favorite by shifting your eyes left or right to indicate the correct hand. Or you could convey misinformation to a kid you didn't like. It was all very strategic.

Another big game was stoop ball, which used a springy, pink rubber ball. A player faced the steps and threw the ball as hard as he could to make it rebound past the other player. If it didn't make it past the sidewalk or if the other player fielded it, you were out. If he dropped it, you counted the bounces to see how many bases it was good for. If the ball bounced all the way up onto the roof of the theater, it was a home run.

It was also game over until somebody could come up with 15 cents for a new ball. Once a month a theater employee would throw all the balls down, showering anyone lucky enough to be there with a lifetime supply.

When we played street stickball, a manhole cover was home plate and the cars served as bases and foul lines. When the police came by, we all ran like crazy. The cops would confiscate the stickball bat to protect the neighborhood from the ravages of our gang.

Bill and his friends had street lamps and asphalt instead of trees and grass in their playground. Bill shows off his big-boy model tricycle (below), complete with blocks on the pedals so his short legs could reach them.

"FATHER'S INCOME AS A BRICK MASON in the '50s and '60s was dependent on the weather, so my mother, Hazel, sewed many of her own and my sister Gina's clothes to save money," says Dennis Peterson of Taylors, South Carolina. "The results looked just as good as anything she might have bought in a department store."

LOOK WHAT WE CAUGHT

THESE SIBLINGS CARRIED home a stringer full of keepers. Carl Vincent of Medical Lake, Washington, says his uncle John Court took this picture and hundreds more of his family and friends over more than 30 years throughout Washington state.

THE GEORGE STREET GIANTS

A BACKYARD FOOTBALL team poses together in 1945 in Greensburg, Pennsylvania. "We just played among ourselves but had lots of fun," writes James Hanson of Mount Holly, North Carolina. "I'm the tall one in the back." Jack Urban (second from left, bottom row) eventually went on to play quarterback for Penn State.

BIG DAY FOR DRESSING UP

NORTHLAND CENTER in Southfield, Michigan, was the largest open-air mall in the U.S. when it opened in 1954. Standing in front of the mall's whimsical Marshall M. Fredericks-designed *The Boy and Bear* statue in 1957, from left, teens Mary Jo Kelly, Cathy Benkert, Carole Zwick and, kneeling, Carla Aderente say goodbye to eighth grade on graduation day. Carole now lives in Redford, Michigan.

SUMMER FUN

IT GETS VERY HOT in Paso Robles, California, in the summer. For a few minutes, some kids cooled down on the small roller coaster at the Mid-State Fair. "You can tell that they don't seem to mind the heat one bit," says Alan Curtis of Templeton, California.

WHY SO SAD?

TAKEN AT THE YMCA'S CAMP DENT in the Poconos of Pennsylvania in 1939, this photo shows William Hirst of Allentown, left, looking like a sad sack. He and another camper were told to look sad for a photograph used in an article about the end of summer and the start of school.

BABY BUTTERFLY

"**I WAS 4 IN 1949** when my folks enrolled me in the Mildred Holmes Dance Studio in Corvallis, Oregon," says Molly G. Smith, now of Sandy, Oregon. "My mother made my costumes, and I wore pink Capezio toe shoes stuffed with pieces of rabbit fur and lamb's wool to cushion my toes. Now, dancing en pointe isn't taught until a ballerina is at least 10."

POSING AT THE COZY

"**IN THE '50s,** my parents' shop, the Cozy Corner, was a popular place to grab a bite," writes David Forney of Olean, New York. "Elaine Haas, 7, stopped in after her First Communion."

JOINING THE SQUAD

"**WITH HELP FROM MY BIG SISTER TONI,** I made the Pep Cats squad at Monrovia High School in Monrovia, California. Here I am during spring 1973, my junior year," says Malena Phillips, now of Stout, Ohio.

My husband built this playhouse in 1966 in our backyard. As you can see, all the neighborhood kids enjoyed it. That's my daughter Janet wearing glasses.

LUCILLE DUH ◆ PISCATAWAY, NJ

ALL IN THE FAMILY

Reflect on memorable vacations, hilarious mishaps, sacrificial love, cherished traditions and more.

CHAPTER 2

Akers Reunion

Juda remembers all the women and kids lining up for a photo at the 1949 reunion.

Gathering Spot

Family reunions bridge the miles for relatives near and far.

JUDA WOODS-HAMLIN ◆ VINCENNES, IN

Family reunions were an annual affair for the Akers family when I was growing up. We always gathered on the last Sunday in August at a reserved building in Lanterman Park in Bridgeport, Illinois. We looked forward to seeing cousins and family members we hadn't seen all year.

Some of the older folks would arrive early to set up. Others came after church. The meal was always served at 12:30 so everyone could arrive in time to say grace.

The meal was bountiful, and the table groaned with all the food everyone brought to share. Aunt Geneva made her famous chicken and noodles. There was fried chicken with what we called pulley bones. Those were my favorite because after you ate the chicken, you could pull on the wishbone and whoever got the longest side got to make a wish. Plates were heaped with meatloaf, mashed potatoes, home-canned

green beans, summer tomatoes and cucumbers fresh from the garden. Pies and cakes were homemade, not store-bought.

After the meal, it was time for the older relatives to visit. They talked about weddings and shivarees and babies; they talked about gardens and canning and the weather. The young adults played baseball; the teenagers talked about school; younger kids played on the swings and slides. Toddlers ran amok until sleepiness overtook them and they curled up on their mommas' laps.

As time went on the reunions eventually got smaller. Older relatives passed away, younger ones moved and no one was left to organize and preserve the tradition. The last reunion I remember was in 1976, the same year my son was born.

Similar to wishbones and shivarees, reunions like ours may seem out of style today.

Prayers Answered

Don Witten of Columbia, Maryland, says family lore has it that his mother, Mary, had been praying for a girl, but when her sixth child was born, she mistook the umbilical cord for something else. "Oh my God," she cried out. "Another boy." The nurse, Sister Rose Xavier, came to the rescue. "No, Mary, it's a girl. See!" So Mary called her only daughter Rose Mary in the nurse's honor.

Mary Witten (above) in 1926, the year she married. Witten clan (left) in '74—Charles, Walter, Elbert Jr., Robert, Rose Mary and Don. Below, Rose Mary, Robert, Charles, Elbert Jr., Walter and Don pose with their mother (third from right) on Mother's Day 1964.

The highlight of 1957 for Judy Phipps Sipe, right, of Tustin, California, was winning a trip to Disneyland. She and her family, from left, mother Helen, sister Jill and father Guy, flew from Nebraska to experience the happiest place on earth.

Where the Magic Happened

His father helped design the park's futuristic frontier.

LARRY SANDERSON ◆ SMYRNA, TN

When Walt Disney's theme park opened 62 years ago, it was named Disneyland and christened "The Happiest Place on Earth." It was a thrill to behold all the rides and exhibits making Disney's movies, cartoons and characters come to life.

My sister, Diane, and I were treated to an even more special event. Our preview of the park occurred a year earlier than the official opening on July 17, 1955.

Our father, Bob, had been hired as an architect/artist to design some of the buildings in Tomorrowland. One day in 1954, he asked Diane and me to go with him to Walt Disney Studios in Burbank while he met with some of the staff.

There, a staff member showed us how the cartoon cels of famous animation characters were painted and gave us a tour around the studio. We saw where many items for the park were being built. There was the Mark Twain

When Disneyland opened in 1955, Tomorrowland was a peek into the future of 1986. Numerous updates have followed since that time.

All dressed up, Larry, 7 (right); his mom, Mary; and his sister, Diane, 9, visited the Walt Disney Studios in Burbank, California, for a look behind the scenes.

riverboat in pieces, ready to ship. And there were the animals of Adventureland's Jungle Cruise being formcast. (They were a little scary because they all looked so real.) My favorite structure, Rocket to the Moon, featured the rocket standing in front of a dual-domed station with a modern curved facade. I remember seeing the model of the building on my dad's drafting table at home.

During our studio tour we ran into Cubby and Karen, the youngest Mouseketeers from *The Mickey Mouse Club.* They told us that when we reached their age, maybe we could join the club on TV.

Later that day we visited the unopened park, where we walked down unpaved Main Street and saw Sleeping Beauty Castle at the end of the road still wrapped in scaffolding. Workers had a lot to accomplish by opening day so Walt Disney could deliver his sparkle and children of all ages could delight in his vision.

My father got VIP passes for the family to visit the park the day before it opened to the public. My sister and I got to ride everything as many times as we wanted. Because I was a space nut, my favorite rides were all in Tomorrowland—the moon rocket, the Astro-Jets and Autopia, where I drove my own like-real car, designed just for kids, that you maneuvered down an actual paved, curving road.

Thank you, Walt, for making your dream come true for us all.

A Sacrifice for a Daydream Believer

At 13, and living in Auburn, New York, in 1967, I thought I'd never stand a chance of seeing my favorite band, the Monkees.

Well, surprise No. 1: My dad came home with tickets for me, my friend Jill and my mom. Days later, we learned that my cousin was going to the concert in Rochester, too, but by herself. What happened next I still can't believe.

Surprise No. 2: My mother switched tickets with my cousin so we girls could sit together.

Imagine my mom sitting alone with 10,000-plus screaming teenyboppers for two hours. What a true sacrifice!

I remember that after the concert, we had trouble finding each other. We'd been seated on different levels.

The experience taught me that sometimes parents do understand their teenage children—and that a mother will go out of her way to make her child's dream come true.

I have lost both of my beloved parents within the past four years, but the memories of all they did for me will live on forever. Thanks, Mom and Dad!

SUE CLANCY ◆ AUBURN, NY

PARTIES WERE POPULAR with Debra Sepe's family after her dad bought a German-made hi-fi stereo console in 1959. Both of her parents enjoyed music, and Mitch Miller was a family favorite. Debra, now of Yorkville, Illinois, remembers passing out sheet music in her parents' basement in 1968.

Virginia Putnam sat with screaming strangers so Sue (left) could scream with people she knew.

A Flash in the Cans

Her skirt had too much flirt. **SKY GERSPACHER** ◆ LYNNWOOD, WA

My life as an 11-year-old in Morganville, New York, in 1966 revolved around *Dark Shadows*, Snoopy and Linus, my homemade skateboard and, of course, *The Monkees*. I never missed an episode of that show. My best friend, Martha, liked Peter Tork, but for me, no one compared to Davy Jones.

My mother always did our weekly grocery shopping on Friday nights. I had mostly given up going with her, but one Friday, with nothing else to do, I grudgingly agreed. I whined all the way there while she pretended not to hear me.

At the store, I wandered off through the aisles, hoping to find a cereal with a cool toy or mail-in offer, when I noticed a stock boy shelving cans of peaches. He wore bell bottoms under his store apron and a paisley button-down shirt. His brown hair was long—a classic Monkees cut. He stood up and I realized that he looked just like Davy Jones! My heart stopped.

I decided I would go to the bathroom, fix my hair and walk by him again. I smoothed my dress, sucked in my tummy and strolled past him, stopping to pretend to inspect some fruit cocktail.

I could see my mother chatting with another woman in the checkout line. I still had some time. I hurried to make a third pass by the Davy Jones look-alike. I just wanted him to notice me. Maybe he'd think I was cute. This time, I was delighted to see him look right at me, smiling broadly. I blushed and smiled back.

My mother, meanwhile, was no longer chatting and instead was staring at me. In fact, she was waving frantically at me. I took one last look at the beautiful stock boy, then went to my mother, surprised by the look of concern on her face. As soon as I was close enough, she reached behind me and tugged on my skirt.

"Oh honey," she said, "you tucked the entire back of your dress into your underwear."

ILLUSTRATION: MATT ZUMBO

Mom Had Superpowers

My mom, Jeannette Head, always had my back. From age 7, I knew my mother was helping shape my life. She was my first teacher and wanted me to be a teacher. The desire was in my heart, too. Every day after school, I would come home and line up my dolls, my sleeping cat and my brother, Donny; write lesson plans; and teach second grade to them.

My mom stayed home even though it was hard for our family. She had a gift for music. She played the piano and organ in church, led the junior choir and taught me to play piano. She created beautiful artwork for our home, kept us healthy by exercising and riding bikes with us, and helped me with my homework.

She used her superpowers to make me the woman I am today. She will always be my childhood hero.

KATHLEEN McDONALD ◆ WATERFORD, PA

MAY 1960

(Above) Kathy's mom, Jeannette, taught piano and sixth-grade Sunday school. Here, Kathy, 8, and her mom take a spin around the backyard of their home in Albion, Pennsylvania.

Arlene, holding the cookbook, was active in her high school Future Homemakers of America classes.

Many Miles from Home

Duty called after a long-distance crisis interrupted her high school education. **SANDY WILSON** ◆ LONGVIEW, WA

My mother, Arlene Remmert Steinbeck, has a life story that she doesn't often tell. She was born July 14, 1931, in St. Peter, Illinois, the third of six children in a family of three girls and three boys.

Her father started work on a farm in Peoria before changing jobs and working for Caterpillar Inc. The family moved to Eureka, Illinois, so he could be closer to the plant. When Arlene was a senior in high school, Caterpillar offered her dad a job that required moving to California. So the entire family relocated, leaving Arlene and her older married sister Berdina behind.

Arlene stayed with family friends Dr. and Charlotte Barker so she could finish at her high school. She baby-sat for their two children in exchange for room and board. The doctor had attended Eureka College, where he became friends with Ronald Reagan. Over the years Reagan was a guest at the Barker house. My mom liked to joke that she'd slept in the same bed as Ronald Reagan.

In spring 1949, Arlene got word that her mother had been hit by a bus and died, so she and her sister boarded a train for San Leandro, California, where the family was living. After the funeral, Arlene returned to Eureka to finish the school year. Dr. Barker offered to pay for her to attend Eureka College, but Arlene knew that her family in California needed her.

She returned to San Leandro to help raise her three younger brothers and got a job working for General Motors. In 1952, she married my father, Warren Steinbeck. The skills she learned from her travels and experiences have helped her throughout her life.

1948

Nourishing MEAT

...a complete protein food

Nourishing meat and a dash of spice—that's what franks are made of. And what are boys and girls made of? Well, protein, of the kind that all meat has, furnishes the "building blocks" for their tissues, muscles, good red blood. So isn't it good that as thrifty a meat as the friendly frank can do the same "nourishment" job for youngsters—and all of us—as the more costly cuts?

P.S. To help you meet food problems, listen to the Food Waking Hour, NBC stations, Tuesday and Thursday mornings.

AMERICAN MEAT INSTITUTE
Headquarters, Chicago • Members throughout the U. S.

THRIFTY TASTE (ABOVE): This 1948 ad from the American Meat Institute highlights hot dogs as a protein-packed, inexpensive meal that can provide "the same 'nourishment' job for youngsters...as the more costly cuts."

LEARNING AT THE HANDS OF A MASTER (BELOW): Swift's created this dynamic print ad. The promo appeared in Life magazine just before the new year, when families would be likely to splurge on a massive rib roast.

1960

Can you remember the first time you carved a big, juicy, standing-rib roast? Chances are it, too, was Swift's Premium. For this wonderful, flavorful beef has been a treat at American dinner tables for generations. It's just one of the superb meats nature blessed with complete, high-quality meat protein—and Swift is proud to bring to your table. It's another example of the extra goodness, extra value you always get for your money, when the label says....

Swift's Premium

...the two most trusted words in meat. Our 106th year.

A Cooked-Up Scheme Falls Flat

He'd soon be eating his words, along with the cake.

PAUL KIEFFER ◆ NORTH CANTON, OH

A big chocolate cake should be all it takes to make a 10-year-old boy happy on his birthday, but this cake turned out to be food for thought that lasted a lifetime.

It all began on the morning of my birthday, June 2, when my mother ordered a chocolate cake from our neighborhood bakery. She asked my friend and me to pick it up before noon. She told us to walk there, but we rode our bikes instead, which turned out to be a big mistake.

> *She told us to walk to the bakery, but we rode our bikes, which turned out to be a big mistake.*

As we rode to the bakery, we were having fun tossing a ball back and forth between us. We could easily ride no-handed—without holding onto the handlebars—a skill we'd mastered after much practice.

We picked up the cake and resumed our game of catch as we rode home. I had the cake balanced in one hand and was playing catch with the other. All was going well until I hit a bump in the road—and, of course, I dropped my birthday cake.

Being a quick thinker, I came up with a story that seemed perfectly believable: I told my mother that the lady at the bakery must have handed me the box upside down, causing the icing to be all messed up. My wise mother knew I was lying, but instead of losing her temper, she devised an ingenious answer that put the dilemma back where it belonged—with me.

She told me to return to the store and tell the woman that she'd handed me my cake upside down. Now what was I going to do? I'd be caught in my lie.

So back to the bakery I went, alone this time because my friend had deserted me in my hour of need. There, I informed the baker what she had done. She just smiled and said she'd re-ice the cake if I promised to confess the truth to my mother.

To this day, whenever I eat chocolate cake, I remember my mother giving me that piece of wisdom about telling lies.

Words of Love

After talk with Mom, son soon realized why
Dad wouldn't read award-winning essay.

GENO LAWRENZI JR. ◆ PHOENIX, AZ

When my father found a higher-paying job in a steel mill in Sutersville, Pennsylvania (population 976), our family's lives changed dramatically for the better.

However, the one thing I don't remember my father ever saying is "I love you." I had two younger brothers and a sister, and I'm pretty sure Dad told my sister he loved her, but I never heard him utter the phrase to me or my brothers.

Because I was an avid reader in grade school, I started writing—short stories, articles and essays—and newspapers and magazines starting buying them to publish. Around 1956, one of my essays, "The American Way," earned me a medal and an honorable mention from the Freedoms Foundation in Valley Forge.

When the medal and a copy of a magazine containing the essay arrived, I ran from the post office to show it to my family. My mother was overjoyed. As for Dad, he retired to the living room to watch TV news.

I had just turned 18. This was the biggest event in my life, and my own father was acting as if it was nothing! That hurt, and I turned to my mother for comfort.

"Sometimes he acts like my talents and I don't exist," I complained. "I tried to show him my essay and he wouldn't even look at it."

"Have a seat," she said. We talked for a long time, and when she was finished, I cried. "Your father can't read, son," was what she said.

I went back to my room, wondering how I could have been so self-centered. I had the magazine with my essay in my hand. That's when I knew what I had to do.

Dad was in the garage working on his car. He was wearing his red baseball cap and his face was grease-stained. I approached him quietly.

"Dad, I'd like to read you something, if you don't mind. It's an essay that I wrote for the Freedoms Foundation. They sent me a medal for it."

"They sent you a medal for writing an essay?"

I showed him the medal. "Would you like to hear it?"

"Sure. Read it to me," he said.

My dad listened attentively as I read the essay. When I was finished, he said he liked it.

"Can I take it to the guys down at the Moose Club to show it to them?" he asked. "I think they'd like to hear what you say about patriotism and the American way."

"Sure, Dad," I said, handing him the magazine. "You can...you can show..." I'm afraid I didn't finish the sentence. It's pretty hard to talk with tears streaming down your face. But I know my father understood me perfectly.

BOOKS: BINH THANH BUI/SHUTTERSTOCK

SKIING PALS

"HERE IS MY DAD with my brother Jim at Diamond Hill Park in Cumberland in 1959," writes Christine Tremblay of Cumberland, Rhode Island. "From the looks on their faces, I can't help but wonder if they were reconsidering tackling the intermediate hill."

More Bounce than Bad Luck

Friday the 13th delivered an unexpected surprise.

DARLENE BLACK ◆ MONTEVIDEO, MN

Friday, Sept. 13, 1935, will always be a most memorable day for me. All was well in my sleepy hometown of Wegdahl, Minnesota. That's where I lived with my parents, Gustav and Mildred Nyheim, and my brother, Ordell, 9. I was 7 and delighted that Grandmother Baxter was staying for a two-week visit.

Around dusk, the adults told my brother and me to go outside to play. This time of day, we usually were called home, so it seemed odd. But I was having fun with a playmate in her yard, so I paid no mind until I noticed the shiny black car in our driveway.

I thought it must be my Great-Aunt Helena from Granite Falls, Minnesota, so I went home to check. I got just inside the door before my father stopped me. Suddenly I heard my mother scream, and I started to cry. "Is Mama dying?" I asked.

"No, no," Dad said to calm me down. The next thing I heard was a cry. I joyously shouted, "Oh, it's a baby!"

Soon we got to see our beautiful newborn baby brother, Paul, who had curly hair with ringlets down the back of his head.

As you may have guessed, the car in the driveway wasn't my great-aunt's; it belonged to the doctor.

Paul hadn't been a tot too long before my father announced, "He's a boy and he has to have a haircut." Off to the barbershop they went. That was a sad day for Mother and me.

But I'll always think of Friday the 13th as a wonderful good-luck day.

> *Suddenly I heard my mother scream, and I started to cry. 'Is Mama dying?' I asked.*

Darlene's brother Paul got a haircut soon after this family photo was taken. Paul has those curls (below) still—in a little brown box tied with a ribbon.

Like Having Two Dads

Her love of dance created a second family.

JEANNIE TUCKER ◆ TUCSON, AZ

Each day after my dad got off work, I would choreograph and perform shows for my parents, James and Frances Tucker. It was obvious to them that I wanted to dance, so they went looking for a teacher for me. That's how my career as a working actor began in the '60s, when I was only 3.

They found Joe Michaels, a widely known dancer, actor and choreographer with studios in New York and Miami. Joe was an original Marlboro Man, a persona created in the 1950s by Leo Burnett as part of a marketing campaign for Marlboro cigarettes. Joe and I signed with the Coronet Modeling Agency in Miami, Florida, and were frequently paired in commercials as a father-and-daughter dance team. We certainly looked the part, and he was a great mentor for me. I could imitate Joe so well, and we loved to dance together.

My father took photos for the dance studio. Dad was a design engineer with a talent for photography and found it a wonderful way to show his support. Dad had a darkroom at home; the red light on the outside of the door signaled when he was working and I couldn't come in. When it was off, it was OK to enter the room.

Our families also became close friends. Joe and his wife and children lived on a houseboat during the '60s when some terrible hurricanes came through the area. My father would help secure their boat and the whole family would stay at our house to weather those storms.

My dad was a combat engineer in the war and so talented he could make something out of nothing. He built the homes we lived in including the plumbing, electrical and everything else. He even built an in-ground swimming pool using an aircraft refueling tank as a pool heater. During one hurricane, Joe's houseboat sank, and my dad helped raise and rebuild it for Joe and his family.

Chief Warrant Officer James W. Tucker (top photo), Jeannie's father, was among the troops who landed on Omaha Beach during the D-Day invasion of France, and showed Jeannie and her mom (on floor at left) his D-Day landing spot. In step with her instructor, Joe Michaels, Jeannie (dancing above) pivots while keeping her eyes on her father, who is taking the photo.

FUN AT THE LAKE

AT A SMALL LAKE IN CALIFORNIA, Rosalie Thompson swings her daughter Darlene in 1947. "This image brings back memories of my mother's love," says Darlene Van Hemelryck of Page, Arizona, "and also of my talented father, Alec, who not only took the picture, but developed and printed it in a darkroom that he built."

CABIN SUMMERS

GERTRUDE WOEHRLIN'S kids Beverly, Kevin and Patricia—along with Simon the Cat—have a snack on the wagon at the family's lakefront cabin. "We moved to the lake the day school was out and didn't move home until school started in fall," she says.

FAMILY DAY AT THE PARK

"FLYING HIGH, my mother, Rose, and I smile for the camera on the umbrella ride in 1968 at Idora Park in Youngstown, Ohio," writes Susan Dietrich of Monaca, Pennsylvania. "My father, Frank, the photographer, was riding in the seat behind us with one of my siblings. Spending a day at one of the many amusement parks nearby was a perfect mini vacation for our big family."

QUITE THE HAUL

"MY HUSBAND, BOB (left), his nephew Dennis McClanahan and Dennis' dad, Dave, caught these fish on a trip in the Colorado Rockies," says Marlene Barnes of Tulsa, Oklahoma. "I like to think their different hats gave them good luck."

CAN I GET A SADDLE?

WHILE AT HER GRANDPARENTS' farm in Adams County, Pennsylvania, Roxie Kump looks ready to hop on Duke for a trot around in May 1965. And the chickens look ready to follow! Roxie's mother, Joan C. Kump of Gettysburg, Pennsylvania, sent in this photo.

PERFECT SUMMER DAY

ON AN AFTERNOON OUTING with his three kids in 1965, Donald Malone of Leesburg, Texas, holds baby John while daughter Michele gives his leg a bear hug. Kathleen looks as though she's seriously contemplating a swim in the water at Riverside Park in Riverside, California. Wife and mother Lillian took the photo.

ALL IS CALM

TAKING A BREAK FROM PADDLING, Bruce Thompson of Waukesha, Wisconsin (right), and his son Steve were in the Boundary Waters Canoe Area in northern Minnesota in 1971. They enjoyed the weeklong camping trip together.

TABLE TALK

A FAMILY ENJOYS A PICNIC in this photo submitted by Carl Vincent of Medical Lake, Washington. His uncle John Court took the photo in 1959.

AFTERNOON PICNICS

WENDELL GLADSTONE, foreground, and his family enjoy lunch in upstate New York in 1936. Among those with him is his wife, Ruth, holding baby Shirley on her lap (back right). Shirley's daughter, Wendy Eaton of Seattle, Washington, sent in the picture.

MILK. IT DOES A BODY GOOD.

JERRY BERTRAM, now of Eau Claire, Wisconsin, says Sealtest brand milk sponsored this photo taken in 1950 of his family in their Highland Heights, Kentucky, kitchen. His mom, Loretta, pours glasses of milk and serves snacks to him and his five brothers, from left, David, Ralph, Donald holding Jerry on his lap, Charlie and Jimmy.

LIVE REPTILES

ALLIGATORS IN FENCED-IN PITS once gave rides to kids at the California Alligator Farm. Located across the street from Knott's Berry Farm in Buena Park, California, the Alligator Farm also housed turtles, ostriches and snakes. Here, grandparents Margie and Jess Doty stand by as Billy the gator provides a seat for Genene Doty Staats of Agua Dulce, California, who submitted the photo, and her brother, Dennis.

NOT JUST FOR THE BIRDS

BACK IN 1968, the Norton clan took over the Noonan Park "duck house," a kids' favorite at this Minnesota lake where waterfowl migrate each year, says Jim Norton of Alexandria, Minnesota.

Chores Were a Way of Life

During the Depression, working was a way of life on our 10-acre farm in what was called the Harmony District in Clark County, Washington. My dad, Bill Stevens, worked at the paper mill for 37 cents an hour. My mom, Violet, kept the home fires burning. My siblings—Shirley, Velma, Ivena, Wilma and Roy—and I worked to pay for school clothes, books and anything else we needed. We went barefoot all summer to save our shoes for the next school term.

Besides the regular farm chores of milking cows and stacking hay, we collected night crawlers in the summer. My dad sold them to fishermen.

Sometimes Dad would take us to the woods to cut fir trees for winter fuel. There we were, my sister and I, ages 12 and 13, pulling a 6-foot crosscut saw. At least we had strong arms.

Somehow we survived falling out of trees and other mishaps, then went on to graduate. The farm life taught us good work habits and provided year-round jobs.

ROBERTA CORLEY-HEIM
WASHOUGAL, WA

Roberta holds her daughter, Linda Corley, in a 1946 Stevens family portrait.

MAKING FRIENDS

HUGGING A PIG, Julie Natale Mann of Centennial, Colorado, makes the most of her family's 1962 trip to Disneyland. Julie's parents drove her and her brother, Kim, from Denver to Los Angeles in a 1960 Chevrolet Impala sedan with an Airstream trailer hitched to the back.

"I love how my mom and dad, Doris and Jim Carroll, used this old box to make a sleigh seat for my brother Eddie, 16 months, in Rosedale, New York, in 1947."

DORIS MAIORINO
NORTH BABYLON, NY

TRUE LOVE

Sometimes steadfast love pops up by surprise or overcomes great distance and difficulties, but it's always sweet.

CHAPTER 3

The 'No' Girl Says Yes

One Valentine's Day changed everything.

JACK JOSEPH • SCOTTSDALE, AZ

Home from the Navy in 1947, I started school at Greenville College in my hometown of Greenville, Illinois, about 50 miles east of St. Louis, Missouri. I had been out of high school for four years, but my high school principal, Mr. Gardner, invited me to a Valentine's Day dance at school. We lived in a small community, and the thought of seeing my former teachers was intriguing. So I agreed.

When Friday came, I cleaned up, gussied up and drove to the high school gym. I chatted with my former teachers and approached Mr. Gardner to thank him before leaving. Just then, the band started playing and a young woman stood up to sing. One look at her and I was mesmerized. I had never seen such a beautiful woman, so I concluded that she must be from a nearby town.

I asked Mr. Gardner who she was, and he answered, "That's Marilyn Riley, Cut Riley's daughter."

I was flabbergasted to say the least. The Rileys lived just around the corner from me.

I walked across the gym floor to introduce myself and said, "Hi, I'm Jack Joseph."

"I know who you are," was her not-too-friendly response.

"Would you like to dance?" I asked.

"No!" she shot back.

"Why not?"

"I'm working," she replied.

"Can I call you next week for a movie date?" I asked.

"No," was her response.

I could see no reason to argue, so I thanked her for nothing, tucked my pride in my coat pocket and left.

For the next month I phoned, trying to set up a date. She always had the same answer: No.

Then one rainy afternoon in March as I was driving home after basketball practice, I saw Marilyn, the "No" girl, walking with no umbrella, no raincoat, no hat.

I pulled alongside her and asked if she needed a ride, half expecting her to say no. Instead, she stepped over the curb and plopped down on the seat next to me. It was only a few blocks to her house, but after pulling into her driveway we talked for 45 minutes. It was magic from that moment on.

Valentine's Day will always hold a special place in my heart. The most beautiful woman I'd ever seen eventually became mine.

Valentine's Day holds a special place in Jack's heart. That's when he met his wife-to-be, Marilyn.

Grammar School Sweethearts Reunite

> *I had never been kissed like that before. I completely forgot my boyfriend's name.*

Frances Stalsworth (left) knew it when she saw Tommy (top and bottom) after all those years. "I hit the jackpot," she says.

My sister Marion and I were invited to a friend's birthday party in 1947. My boyfriend planned to meet me there. (He later called to say he couldn't make it. Talk about luck.)

When I arrived, a young man opened the door. He was the most handsome man I had seen in my 16 years—with a black crew haircut, a small mustache and beautiful blue eyes. His name was Tommy. "He's mine," I whispered to Marion.

After the party started, we played post office. I was extremely shy, but I cheated and got Tommy's number, 13. Before I could call it, he called my number, 10. (I later learned that he had cheated, too.) I had never been kissed like that before. I completely forgot my boyfriend's name.

When refreshments were served, Tommy offered me a taste of his ice cream. He sat with me and asked if he could take me home.

I agreed, and when we got to my house, I started to introduce him to my parents but had to ask his last name. The minute he said "Stalsworth," I realized he had been my sweetheart in second grade.

Back then, our teacher made double rows, and my desk was adjacent to Tommy's. One day, Tommy brought in a small glass lamb and placed it on his desk. He slowly pushed it onto my desk and whispered, "It's yours." Then he kissed me on the cheek and ran into the coatroom. Soon afterward, I changed schools and lost touch with him, but I had thought about him often.

Tommy and I waited until I was 18, in 1949, to get married, and we had four daughters and a son. Our wonderful marriage lasted almost 57 years, until his death in 2006.

FRANCES STALSWORTH ◆ CORRYTON, TN

Night School Sparked a Six-Decade Romance

You just never know when and where you might meet the love of your life.

WARREN S. PATRICK ◆ TOWNSHEND, VT

The Monday after I graduated from Central High School in Springfield, Massachusetts, in 1929, I went to work in a hardware store in Springfield about 3 miles from Sixteen Acres, a small community where we lived.

I wanted to go to college, so I had taken a college-prep course in school. The Great Depression was approaching, however, and I knew I would not be able to both work and go to college. Instead, I took a two-year business course in night school learning typing and bookkeeping. That course helped me all my working life, including 27 years later when I became the town clerk and treasurer of Jamaica, Vermont, for 11 years.

While in night school, I noticed Phyllis, an attractive young woman taking a high school diploma course. She had to leave day school to care for her invalid mother, and she wanted her diploma. Being shy, I asked if I could walk her home, and she agreed. We became good friends, and I even brought her to visit with my family.

Two years later, both my father and I lost our jobs. My parents, two sisters and I were forced to move into a crudely altered two-car garage. My older siblings had married and moved to Hartford, Connecticut. Because there was no room for me inside the garage, I slept on the ground-level open porch for two years.

When our car was repossessed, one of my married sisters invited us to move in with her and her husband. As soon as we were settled, I found a job with Firestone Tire & Rubber Co. With a steady income, I asked Phyllis to join me, which she did. We eloped and found a nearby apartment of our own.

Some 60 years later, I was surprised to learn that my father and mother had done the same in 1886 by driving a horse and buggy to the nearest town.

Love Behind the Iron Curtain

If at first you don't see sparks, just wait. **WYNNE CROMBIE** ◆ HUNTLEY, IL

The Cold War was in full swing in August 1967, and there I was, 92 miles behind the Iron Curtain, working for the U.S. Air Force as a teacher at the base school in Berlin. I had just finished two years at Aviano Air Base in Italy.

Before I could even reach my new destination about 90 minutes from the eastern edge of West Germany, I was subjected to a mandatory lecture from U.S. forces at the East/West German border crossing. They informed me about towers, searches and warnings, and what could happen if I took the wrong turn.

I might have turned back then and there. It's a good thing I didn't, because that decision determined my future.

Two weeks into my foray, I met Jack, one of the base lawyers, at a party. We hit it off, and he invited me to another party the following Saturday at the Air Force bachelor officers' quarters in Tempelhof. Of course I'd go!

When I arrived, I stood impatiently in the crowded room full of American personnel and German stewardesses. No Jack. As I tapped my foot, a young man strolled across the room, and I accidentally tripped him.

"Oh my goodness, I'm so sorry!"

"No, no. It's my fault. Er, where are you from?"

"Tacoma, Washington. And you?"

"Philadelphia."

And so it began. Real sparks? No. Not at that time. He said his name was Kent, Kent Crombie. It was an inauspicious beginning. But the next evening he came over and helped me grade arithmetic papers.

Somehow, over the following weeks, love just crept up on us. I remember him talking to me as we danced to a string trio at the British Officers' Club, and the thought came to me: You can tell me later, after we're married.

The Officers' Club Ball was coming up on Dec. 16. I bought the most elegant fabric I could find plus a Burda pattern (German fashion at the time) and made my dress.

We got engaged during a slow waltz.

The following Feb. 3, 1968, we were married in Tacoma and honeymooned in Carmel, California.

The couple (above) holds part of the fallen Berlin Wall. In 2011 Wynne (left) visited a replica of the Checkpoint Charlie guardhouse with Kent when they eventually returned to Berlin.

Not Your Typical Romeo

Luckily, their marriage overcame the challenges of the honeymoon.

NORMAN KAY • ELKINS PARK, PA

Our honeymoon started on June 21, 1947, at the Drake Hotel in Philadelphia, Pennsylvania. I woke up in the middle of the night to a hard push from my new wife and wound up on the floor. I remember thinking to myself, *Is there an unspoken message here?*

The next morning Sandy and I boarded a train to Miami Beach, Florida. When the conductor asked for our tickets, I handed him our marriage license by mistake. He looked at me and said, "This is good for a lot of rides, but not on this train. You'll have to produce a ticket."

Later that morning, after ordering pancakes in the dining car, a woman across the table asked why I was pouring coffee on my pancakes. "It isn't coffee; it's syrup," I replied. "They probably heat it up to make it pour easier." Well, I was wrong and she was right. It was coffee.

Sandy and Norman had a series of stumbles, but their love stayed strong.

> *The clerk told me that they didn't have a double bed but that I could push together the two singles.*

When we pulled into Fort Lauderdale and went to our hotel, another surprise awaited—twin-size beds. I immediately called the desk and told the clerk I was on my honeymoon and definitely had ordered a double bed. The clerk told me that they didn't have a double bed but that I could push together the two singles. I raised my voice and said, "I want what I ordered." A double bed was delivered—at 6:30 the next morning.

Things were definitely starting to add up, and after I mistakenly used Vaseline instead of underarm deodorant, my lovely new bride expressed a look of concern about our lifelong commitment.

Sure enough, when we returned to Philadelphia, I sprained my back carrying her across the threshold of our new home and spent two weeks in bed.

That was 68 years ago, and I don't put coffee on my pancakes or Vaseline under my arms anymore. But after reviewing what I wrote here, a second honeymoon would be most welcome.

Susan knew that a wedding didn't have to be very big for her and Norm to be happy.

Brother, Can You Share a Friend?

During the height of WWII, my brother Harry became friends with Norm Walter when they were stationed in the 908th Ordnance at Dawson Creek, British Columbia.

One day, Harry showed Norm a photo of me. After that, Norm wrote me a letter. I answered, and for a full year we exchanged letters and photos back and forth.

When the soldiers got furloughs, my brother brought Norm home for a visit. After a year of corresponding, I finally got to meet Harry's good friend in March 1944. Norm was thoughtful, considerate, polite and handsome.

Soon we were engaged and got married. Two months later, he was shipped to Germany, which meant another year of letter writing for us before that beautiful Christmas Day in 1945 when he was discharged.

For nearly 70 years, the friend that Harry shared with me was my one true love.

SUSAN WALTER ◆ ST. JOSEPH, MO

IT WAS ONLY puppy love for Ardella Score of Minot, North Dakota, who saved her grade school Valentine's Day cards from the 1940s. Children exchanged the cards during school parties.

SHE CAUGHT MY EYE at a square dance in Dayton, Ohio, where we both had gone alone. Her name was Rosemary Ann Wheelock, and we ended up going home together. I asked her to go to a concert the next day at Deeds Carillon, a tower on the riverbank.

Every Sunday afternoon a musician played a concert on its bells. Beautiful! We were sitting on the grass when I spotted a fat worm crawling on her pretty blue jumper. I reached for it and squished it into a big greenish yellow blob on her dress.

Later we stopped at the Virginia Cafeteria, a popular downtown eatery. She couldn't get the ketchup out of the bottle, so I grabbed it and whacked the bottom. Half its contents landed on her dress.

I figured she'd never see me again, but here are pictures of us then and now, after almost 69 years of marriage—and some stain remover.

ALLAN YOUNG ◆ LAWRENCE, KS

As Ernie and Lavaughn rode the chairlift up the hill in 1955, a photographer strapped to one of the poles took their picture.

We Met on a Ski Lift

My wife, Lavaughn Gordanier, and I met 65 years ago on the chairlift at Mammoth Mountain, California. She was skiing with her brother and his business partner. I was skiing with a couple of buddies and all of us were from Los Angeles.

The 1955 season was extremely busy because it was the first year the No. 1 chairlift was installed, resulting in long lines. The chairs were two-seaters, so the wait was about 45 minutes. I was ending a run and approached the crowd that was waiting to get on the chairlift. I yelled "Single," hoping someone would raise a hand and I wouldn't have to wait so long.

Lavaughn was in the front of the line, waiting with her brother and his business partner. The two of them were getting a seat together, so she yelled "Single" and held up her hand. I quickly made my way around the crowd, stepped in line, and proceeded to the lift.

After a few rides, Lavaughn and I discovered that we had gone to the same high school, had both been involved in Scouting in our teens, and had camped in the same cabin in the foothills near Sierra Madre on different weekends. We were both in our 20s and realized we had a lot in common.

We were soon married and had a skiing honeymoon in Sun Valley, Idaho. The snow was poor for skiing, so we went back to California and Mammoth Mountain.

In the ensuing years, we have skied at every resort in California, a few resorts in other states, and in Austria and Germany. We love to ski, love the snow and love each other.

ERNIE OGREN ◆ TORRANCE, CA

Love Letters to Treasure

Hidden for years, hundreds of notes are uncovered by daughter.

CAROLE WEBB SLATER ◆ FRANKLIN, TN

> 66 *I come in from flying and I'm all pooped out, then I read a letter from you and I'm not so tired anymore. I love you more than I thought was possible to love anyone.* 99

Cobby and Evelyn's courtship started like many others: An aviation cadet stationed in Nashville attends a USO dance and is attracted to a young lady with an engaging smile and spirited personality. He introduces himself, they dance the night away and go on a few dates before he ships out to Maxwell Air Force Base in Alabama.

A very genuine and passionate man, Cobby, my father, had heartfelt emotions and lots to say. He wrote my mother, Evelyn, frequently. As the months went by, the young couple revealed themselves to each other in written words. Over time, a much deeper love emerged.

One Sunday night, after a sweet weekend visit to Alabama, Evelyn decided not to board the homeward-bound train and eloped with Cobby. A few months later, he left for England as a P-51 fighter pilot in the 352nd Fighter Group flying missions over Germany. For the next 18 months, there were more letters.

Although my father survived World War II, he died 10 years later in a plane crash. As a young girl, I remembered him through stories told by my mother and grandmother.

In 1988, after my mother died, I discovered 250 love letters she had gotten from him. For more than three decades and through multiple moves, she had carried those letters concealed in an obscure chest. My grandmother also saved her son's letters to her during that time.

My family will cherish the legacy of my father's written words forever.

Carole's father, Cobby (top), had two loves: airplanes and his wife, Evelyn (below). Ruth Evelyn Webb kept Cobby's letters tied up in boxes at the bottom of her hope chest.

Just Clowning Around

Step right up for a tale of circus adventure.

DEBBIE KOOP ♦ LAKEWOOD, CO

> For me, it was love at first sight—even though I didn't know what Scott really looked like.

On my 20th birthday my family went to see the circus in Anaheim, California. The girls who wore those beautiful costumes and rode the elephants fascinated me. Because I had been a dancer for many years, I couldn't help but wonder what it would be like to travel with "The Greatest Show on Earth."

Two days later I read in the paper that the Ringling Bros. and Barnum & Bailey Circus was holding auditions in Los Angeles for showgirls. I went to the tryouts just for fun, but I did so well I ended up in Florida to start rehearsals. I learned the web, an aerial ballet performed 30 feet above the audience, and how to dance while wearing a fancy 2-foot-tall headpiece. I was also taught to perform tricks with my elephant, Sara (pronounced Zara in German), alongside the famous animal trainer Gunther Gebel-Williams.

Then in 1981, I met Scott during a show at Madison Square Garden in New York City. Scott always loved clowning around, so after high school he applied to Ringling's Clown College. There he developed his own clown character and skits while learning to juggle, ride a unicycle, walk on stilts, apply makeup and build props. After graduating, he joined the team in the spring of 1981 and got to perform with the famous clown Lou Jacobs.

For me, it was love at first sight—even though I didn't know what Scott really looked like. Every time I saw him he had on his red wig, big nose and clown costume. I fell in love with his personality.

We were married in 1985 and just celebrated our 31st wedding anniversary. I cherish the wonderful memories I have of my time spent with the circus, and I could not imagine what life would be like if I had not met Scott. I am so lucky to have met the greatest husband on Earth while working for the greatest show.

Debbie and Scott Koop performed in the Ringling Bros. and Barnum & Bailey Circus.

Driven Together

She had a Camaro. He had a Charger. Ain't love a gas?

MURLEEN GOODRICH ◆ DELTA, CO

Back in 1970, my parents helped me buy a green 1967 Camaro RS. I loved shifting gears and feeling the power of the 327 engine. It was a good thing I was working. Keeping my Camaro in gas was a challenge, with its four-barrel carburetor and the way I enjoyed speed. The fastest I ever went was 110 mph, and although the car could go faster, I lacked the courage to push it.

One Friday night I was "dragging the gut," which was our term for driving up and down Main Street in Canon City, Colorado, when I stopped for a red light and looked over at the car beside me. It was a 1969 white Dodge Charger that was lookin' real good, and with a very handsome pair of hands resting on the steering wheel.

The driver looked over and met my gaze. I smiled, and he dipped his head slightly. At the next red light he asked me if I'd like to ride with him, so I decided to park my Camaro and get into his Charger.

There was an instant rapport between us, and we ended up talking until 3 a.m. I had to be at work at 5 a.m., so we made a date for that night. Then he went back to Fort Carson, where he was stationed, and I went home to get ready for work. I was so excited I never felt tired. I worked my shift with wings on my feet.

His name was Dale, and we began keeping steady company, never running out of things to talk about. He could always make me laugh, and my whole world just sparkled.

We loved our cars. So many of our dates included adventures with our cars. One afternoon we were driving back to Canon City from Colorado Springs, and I decided to see if he could keep up. The road was fun, the sky clear blue, and I was laughing as he stayed right on my tail. I glanced down at my speedometer, noticed it registered 90 mph, and looked up to see that Dale had dropped back and that a cop was behind me with his lights on. Feeling foolish and doomed, I pulled over. The officer walked up to my car and, pointing back at Dale, asked, "Is that fellow bothering you?"

"No sir," I said quietly. "I know him. We're friends." The officer went back to his squad car, and I got on the road again, driving a sedate and

Murleen married Dale, the man in the white Charger, in 1971.

legal speed the rest of the way home.

Dale and I became serious, much to my parents' dismay. They didn't approve of him and thought they could get me to change my mind if they took away my Camaro. They were paying the insurance on the car because my paycheck wouldn't cover my rent and car payment, plus insurance and necessities. But I didn't even have to think about it.

I handed over the keys.

This year, Dale and I celebrated our 46th anniversary. I've never had any regrets.

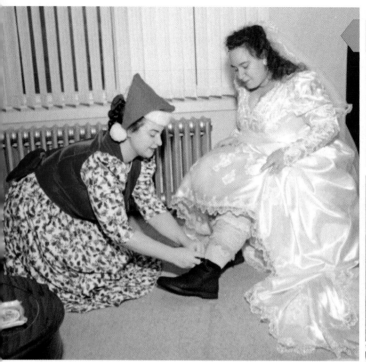

SHE TIED THE KNOT

WHEN IT WAS TIME for Rita Reali of Crossville, Tennessee, to get married, matron of honor Mary Bach tied her snow boots so her wedding shoes wouldn't get ruined in a December storm.

TWO HEARTS BEAT AS ONE

FREDERICK STRASSBURGER'S PARENTS, Robert and Clara, were married in St. Joseph Catholic Church in Peoria, Illinois, on June 26, 1948. Trailing tin cans tied to their bumper announced to all that a wedding had taken place that day.

A SNOWY SHOOT

FOR THEIR ENGAGEMENT picture, Billie and Bob Davenport pose in Bethel, Vermont, in 1955. "My mother was from New England, but my dad was a Floridian and had never seen snow before," says their daughter, Bobbie Davenport of Huntsville, Alabama. "He fell in love with the white stuff and played in it every day. The dogs were my mother's; she'd had them since they were puppies."

NOT GETTING ANY YOUNGER

RUTH ESTHER DEIHM and her beau, John Rutherford Phillips, loved cruising through the West End neighborhood of Norristown, Pennsylvania, back in the Roaring Twenties. But it had been eight years, and upon hearing that her much-younger sister was getting married at age 19 on Feb. 24, 1934, Ruth had a fit, according to her niece Ruthmarie Brooks Silver of Eagleville. So Ruth and John rushed to get married two months sooner, on Ruth's birthday, Dec. 2.

ATTENTION SHOPPERS

RICHARD AND SALLIE PRICE seal it with a kiss at Vern's Shopping Center in Oakland, California. The couple won a contest to marry at the store in 1954.

LAYERED IN LASTING LOVE

LARGE CAKES WERE QUITE UNUSUAL when Theresa Pipia and Michael Cozza got married in June 1939. "But my grandmother Angelina Pipia had her mind set," says Janet Kielas of Milwaukee, Wisconsin. "After a private in-home consultation, she ordered my mother and father's wedding cake from an Italian bakery in the Third Ward in Milwaukee. The baker made an amazing cake using decorative pillars as supports between layers of the towering confection."

'I've Been Right Here'

A story my family tells often is how my mom, Charmaine, and my dad, Wayne, became pen pals and fell in love while he was in the Army in Korea in 1951. But there's much more to the tale.

While overseas, Dad's buddy Otis carried a picture of his girl, Clarabelle, standing beside another woman. He showed the photo to Wayne. Wayne asked about the other woman and learned it was Clarabelle's sister Charmaine. Wayne asked Otis if he thought Charmaine would write to him.

Soon, Wayne and Charmaine were writing back and forth and sending pictures. In one letter Wayne wrote, "I have a question to ask you, but I'm afraid you will say no." Charmaine sent her reply: "Yes, I will marry you."

Remember, they'd never met.

Luckily, she had guessed the right question!

In March 1952, Wayne returned to Missouri on furlough. Charmaine was supposed to take the bus from Alton, Illinois, to Springfield, Missouri, and meet him. From there, they would drive to Mountain Home, Arkansas, with his parents to get married.

Charmaine, who hadn't taken many bus rides, got out at the first bus station in Springfield. She waited and waited but was sure Wayne had stood her up.

Wayne, meanwhile, was across town at the main bus station. He too waited and waited, and also believed he had been stood up. Finally, he got a taxi to go home. First, though, he had to stop at the other bus station to pick up some gear he'd stored in a locker.

The taxi waited as he ran into the station. There she was—the girl in the photo. Charmaine's first words to Wayne were, "Where have you been?" His first to her were, "Where the hell have you been?" Charmaine calmly replied, "Well, I've been right here."

And that is the romantic story of how a soldier and a woman became pen pals, fell in love and agreed to spend their lives together—even though they'd never actually met.

Mom and Dad had four daughters and were married for almost 40 years until Dad passed away on his birthday in 1991.

RHONDA BARCUS ◆ FERNANDINA BEACH, FL

Together at last, Charmaine and Wayne found true romance.

As newlyweds in 1946, my husband, Newton, and I may not have had wealth, but we were oh so happy. Our romance began on a moonlight hike in high school and lasted 55 wonderful years.

GLADYS PIELL ◆ WELLSBORO, PA

FADS, FASHION AND FUN

Trends change, but the memory of feeling up to date never disappears. Take a look back at the entertainment and style crazes that shaped our world.

CHAPTER 4

Bouffants vs. Beehives

Two hairstyles stand out in the world of backcombing and hairspray: bouffants and beehives. Here's how you tell them apart.

- The wide, rounded style made its appearance in the 1950s, thanks to a sticky new product: lacquer hairspray.

BOUFFANT

- Here's how it worked: Women used large wire-mesh rollers and backcombed their hair away from their heads (sometimes adding hairpieces), then flipped the ends up or down. Heavy aerosol hairspray held those voluminous dos in place.

- The bouffant became hugely popular in the early 1960s, thanks to Jackie Kennedy, the always impeccably groomed first lady.

- Other bouffant buffs: Annette Funicello, Mary Tyler Moore, and Diana Ross and The Supremes.

- Beehives: Bouffants gone wild.

- Beehives are styled to soar; bouffants use circumference as their guide.

BEEHIVE

- Invented by Chicago hairstylist Margaret Vinci Heldt, the loftier coif was curled, backcombed and wrapped in a conical shape for its debut in *Modern Beauty Shop* magazine's February 1960 issue.

- Thanks to layers of hairspray and a legion of bobby pins, the glamorous hairdo lasted at least a week if it was wrapped with a scarf at night to protect it.

- Early devotees: Brigitte Bardot, Aretha Franklin, and Audrey Hepburn in *Breakfast at Tiffany's*.

TRENDY COIFS

IN WHITTIER, CALIFORNIA, four cousins pose in their trendy coifs for a family photo in 1967. Raylene Kazarian (left) wears a beehive. Jeannie Kazarian Sogoian (center) boasts a bouffant. At upper right, Donna Naccachian pairs a Sassoon-style haircut with chic sunglasses. And rocking a mop top is Mark Villwock Correy, Donna's brother, now of North Tustin, California.

Claire shown in white lace-up boots and a belted sizzler skirt.

> " *Fifty years ago, syndicated musical variety shows helped popularize go-go boots from coast to coast.* "

SHINDIG! ✦ ABC
SEPTEMBER 1964 TO JANUARY 1966

TV's first prime-time rock-music show featured the top artists of the day, including the Animals, the Byrds and even the Beatles. Soul and R&B stars such as the Temptations, and early rock legends like Jerry Lee Lewis and Little Richard, also got their time in the TV spotlight. The house band was the Shindogs. The Shindig Dancers (10 or so young women) gyrated behind and around the musical acts.

HULLABALOO ✦ NBC
JANUARY 1965 TO APRIL 1966

Hullabaloo boasted a generous budget and a different celebrity host each week, with headliners such as Petula Clark and Frankie Avalon introducing the other performers. The bigger budget also meant bigger props: Imagine watching the Mamas & the Papas—with Michelle Phillips and Mama Cass Elliot in go-go boots—and seeing the Hullabaloo Dancers pop out of claw-foot tubs to do their thing.

WHERE THE ACTION IS ✦ ABC
JUNE 1965 TO MARCH 1967

A spin-off of *American Bandstand*, this Dick Clark-created show took after-school viewers outdoors to watch top hit-makers perform—usually at the beach. Guests included Lesley Gore, Marvin Gaye, the Moody Blues and the Who. The show's house band? Paul Revere & the Raiders (at least through 1966). Pete Manifee and the Action Kids—a troupe of young men and women, often in go-go boots—danced in the background.

Gaga for Go-Go Boots

Hip teens of the 1960s and '70s got their kicks from wearing long, tall, sexy boots. Were you one of them?

CLAIRE CIARLO AUSTIN ✦ FREDERICKSBURG, VA

Boots were definitely the fashion statement when I was a student at Henry C. Conrad High School (Wilmington, Delaware), and I wore go-go boots whenever I could.

Am I gaga for go-go boots? You bet I am! I have about 15 pairs in my closet, and I always will. In fact, I wore them to the high school's All Class Reunion held in April 2016.

While growing up in Delaware, I watched TV shows like *Shindig!* and *Hullabaloo*. I would dance around my house in go-go boots and pretend I was one of the dancers on TV. Attending my high school dances in those beloved boots let me live that fantasy.

1948

N.W. AYER created an illustrated print campaign for Webster Cigars in the 1940s featuring the same couple living it up at chic spots such as Chicago's Pump Room and, in this case, the Boca Raton Club in Florida. Artist Edwin Georgi's mixed-media painting, richer than a photograph, conveys a lush world. The cigar at bottom left seems to be almost an afterthought.

1961

THIS DRAMATIC concept ad by fashion artist Roy Colonna for Galey & Lord, a textiles company, ran in Harper's Bazaar and resembles design sketches found in fashion magazines. Interestingly, designer Pauline Trigère did not sketch her ideas first; she draped and cut directly from fabric bolts.

DISCO DUDS

AFTER DRESSING IN HOT PANTS and suede boots, Renate Smith, now of Milner, Georgia, is clearly ready to go dancing with her husband, Thomas. His version of disco duds included bell-bottoms, a polyester shirt and a gold link bracelet, she recalls. Their favorite dance music? "Knock on Wood" by Eddie Floyd, "That's the Way (I Like It)" by KC and the Sunshine Band, and "Soul Man" by Sam & Dave. "Dancing was a good way to relax after working hard during the week," Renate says.

LEXINGTON BEAUTY

"I KEPT THIS DRESS ALL THESE YEARS because it represents a labor of love from my mother," says Nelle Goff Wheat, shown at 17 wearing the organdy formal her mother created in 1949. Nelle wore the gown in a local Tennessee beauty pageant and at Lexington High School's junior-senior dinner. Today, the dress hangs in her bedroom alongside her grandmother's bed and dresser. "Wonderful memories surround me when I reflect on these things of the past," says Nelle, now of Oakland, Tennessee.

Jeopardy! host Alex Trebek has won five Daytime Emmys over his 33 years on the job, and in 2013, he was inducted into the Broadcasting & Cable Hall of Fame.

I'll Take Frustrated for $200, Alex

It took some practice, but she put in a game performance.

BARBARA PIXLEY • FREDERICKSBURG, VA

My children suggested I try out for *Jeopardy!* I was a college teacher and lived in Calabasas, California, close to Los Angeles, so I thought, *why not?*

These days you take the test online, but in 1990 you had to call the local TV station affiliate to register. There were about 100 people waiting at the test site. They gave each of us a sheet of paper with space for 100 answers, and they warned us that the questions would come very quickly and cover a variety of topics. You had to answer fast, and there was no time to go back if you missed one. About 15 of us made it through that first round.

Next, they divided us into groups of three. They stood us in front of a TV monitor, a school bell in front of each contestant. It was a simulated show, with questions coming up on the monitor. If you knew the answer, you rang the bell as soon as possible. Then they took a photo of each of us and told us to wait for a callback.

> *Press it too early and you'd be blocked out, too late and you'd be beaten.*

A week or so later, I got my call. My appearance was with two other women, and one of them was a returning champion.

The real trick to succeeding at *Jeopardy!* was not just understanding the answer (or "question," in *Jeopardy!* parlance), but also knowing how to play the buzzer. Press it too early and you'd be blocked out, too late and you'd be beaten. The champions have an edge because they've had more practice with the darn buzzer. (Several years later, *Jeopardy!* changed its policy, giving all new contestants a few practice rounds with the buzzer to even their chances.)

I came in second with a score of $12,000, and I got the Final Jeopardy question—"Who is Oprah Winfrey?" After the show aired, friends would hum the *Jeopardy!* theme song whenever I walked into a room.

His Cheatin' Heart Was Impressive

When I was 12, in 1944, I worked as a duckpin setter at a local bowling alley on weekends.

An older pinsetter named Joe played the pinball machines constantly and spent considerable time planning how to beat them. He found a way to save some of his score by pushing quickly on the coin slot every time he put in a nickel. Joe's scores climbed, but not fast enough to satisfy him. So he would lift one end of the machine and put it on the tip of his shoe to reduce the slope, which slowed down the balls. This gave him better control with the flippers, and his score zoomed.

But when the manager caught him in the act, Joe had to come up with a new cheat—and it was a doozy. He drilled a hole in the side of the machine and inserted a bent coat hanger. As a ball came down, hitting bumpers and racking up points, Joe used the hanger to tap one of the bumpers, which dinged with a constant blast of points. We all watched, far too mesmerized to turn Joe in.

It didn't take long for the manager to find out and ban Joe from the machines. But while his streak lasted, Joe impressed us all.

FRED ZOERB ◆ SOMERSET, PA

NUMBERS GAME

1941

The year the first commercial TV game show, *Truth or Consequences*, debuted as an experimental broadcast. The show returned in 1950 for regular daily programming.

....

62

The number of years the longest-running game show, *The Price Is Right*, has appeared on TV.

....

7

The number of *Match Game* versions to air on TV, both as network originals and in syndication. The most recent was the 2016 summer revival on ABC, with host Alec Baldwin.

....

75

The number of consecutive game appearances by *Jeopardy!* contestant Ken Jennings in 2004. His total winnings over 74 games—he lost game 75 to contestant Nancy Zerg—was $2,520,700.

20,000

The number of women *Family Feud* quizmaster Richard Dawson is estimated to have kissed on the show between 1976 and 1985.

FULL TILT

Arcade and video games could keep us out of trouble for hours.

WE FOUND A BETTER USE OF OUR TIME

The first "arcade" game that I played—and the first one I ever saw—was Pong. It wasn't much by today's standards, just a blip bouncing between two lines on a TV screen.

My brand-new bride and I were staying alone at my parents' house (yes, the Pong game belonged to them). We sat on the edge of the bed in front of a portable black-and-white TV and played all three levels before we got completely bored and eventually moved on to other things.

WAYNE TILDEN ◆ ROSEVILLE, CA

BASKETBALL

VIDEO OLYMPICS™

VIDEO PINBALL™

ASTEROIDS™

BREAKOUT™

COMBAT

SPACE INVADERS*

MISSILE COMMAND™

BASIC PROGRAMMING

SKY DIVER™

LASER BLAST™

P

ATARI — X 2624
ATARI — CX 262_
ATARI — CX2648
ATARI® — CX2649
ATARI — CX 2622
ATARI® — CX 2601
ATARI® — CX 2632
ATARI® — CX2638
ATARI — CX 2620
ATARI — CX2629
ACTIVISION — INTERNATIONAL EDITION

KING OF THE JUNGLE

As a simulation engineer in the early 1980s, I did a lot of work at Naval Air Station Cecil Field in Jacksonville, Florida. I often ate at ShowBiz Pizza and then played the arcade games there.

The most popular games at the time were Pac-Man and Donkey Kong, but I spent all my tokens on Jungle King. For me, it was something of an adventure. I got to swing through the trees, being careful to avoid the monkeys; swim across a river, ducking the crocodiles; jump over or evade falling rocks; and eventually save a girl from a boiling cauldron. The kids playing around me were amazed that a grown-up could get as far in the game as I did.

DENNIS KORANEK ◆ MADISON, VA

66 *My mother, Madeline, has always been a technology buff, and in the 1980s she got an Intellivision gaming system. She loved it, particularly the game Advanced Dungeons & Dragons. It was fun to watch her play.* 99

KATHIE WHITE ◆ HASTINGS, MI

INTELLIVISION'S
Advanced Dungeons & Dragons (1982) is an early example of a storytelling adventure game.

••••••••••••••••••••••••••••••••••

THE INVENTION OF
Skee-Ball is usually credited to J.D. Estes of Philadelphia, Pennsylvania, in 1909.

••••••••••••••••••••••••••••••••••

NINTENDO'S SUPER MARIO BROS.
(1985) was the first video game with music created by a professional composer, Koji Kondo.

••••••••••••••••••••••••••••••••••

THE ATARI JAGUAR,
first released in 1993, is now an open platform, which means independent software developers can create and publish games for it without a license.

Monopoly Monkey Business

She didn't stand a chance when her brothers ran the board.

PEGGY TROWSDALE ◆ HADASHVILLE, MB

Growing up in the 1950s and '60s with four siblings gave me many memorable experiences. Playing Monopoly with my two older brothers was just one of them.

While sitting at the kitchen table in our old farmhouse, my brothers taught me everything about board games that our parents didn't want us to know. When we played, Bruce (four years older than me) was the banker and Warren (seven years my elder) was the real estate agent. The cards were stacked against me from the very start.

There was more cheating going on between the two of them than you'd find in a Hank Williams song. My brothers were sneaky, and they'd trade money and property cards under the table. When I wasn't looking, green houses and red hotels would magically appear on their properties. As the clock ticked, the boys got richer while I, their poor—very poor—and naïve little sister, would get closer to bankruptcy.

After spending about an hour trying to prove they were cheating, I'd quit. Then I would exclaim that this was the last game of Monopoly I would ever play with them. Ever.

Inevitably, they would coax me to play again, promising no more monkey business. Over and over, I believed them. We would start another game, but just like a repeat of an old *Three Stooges* episode, the whole circus would start once again.

So much for friendly competition. Today, though it's almost 60 years later, I still shake my head at what a gullible little sister I was!

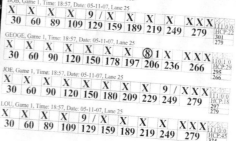

Lou (second from left) and his teammates receive an award from the Massachusetts Bowling Association for setting a one-game scoring record in 2005. The score sheet (below) shows how the team reached its total pin count of 1,103.

PRO LANES
Thank You

11/8/05

BOB, Game 1, Time: 18:57, Date: 05-11-07, Lane 25

| X | X | X | X | 9 | / | X | X | X | X | X | X | X | |
|30|60|89|109|129|159|189|219|249| |279| | | |

HCP-22 / 301 / 279

GEOGE, Game 1, Time: 18:57, Date: 05-11-07, Lane 25

| X | X | X | X | X | X | X | 8 | 1 | X | X | X | X | |
|30|60|90|120|150|178|197|206|236| |266| | | |

HCP-29 / 295 / 266

JOE, Game 1, Time: 18:57, Date: 05-11-07, Lane 25

| X | X | X | X | X | X | X | X | 9 | / | X | X | X | |
|30|60|90|120|150|180|209|229|249| |279| | | |

HCP-18 / 297 / 279

LOU, Game 1, Time: 18:57, Date: 05-11-07, Lane 25

| X | X | X | X | 9 | / | X | X | X | X | X | X | X | |
|30|60|89|109|129|159|189|219|249| |279| | | |

HCP-45 / 324 / 279

Total: 1103, Average: 275

King of the Hill

Bowling alleys in Lawrence, Massachusetts, where I grew up, used either candlepins or duckpins. It wasn't until 1954, when I was assigned to Randolph Air Force Base near San Antonio, Texas, that I was introduced to tenpins. The balls were three times the size and weight of duckpin balls. But I got hooked. I joined many leagues and practiced every day. I even made the base's bowling team.

After I was discharged in 1958, I came home to find several new tenpin bowling alleys in Lawrence and the surrounding area. Within two years, a TV station in Boston was broadcasting a weekly show from Sammy White's Brighton Bowl, which was owned by the former Red Sox catcher. Alleys across the state held qualifying rounds—whoever had the highest score over five games won $200. I won the qualifying round to make it

to my first week of TV competition in December 1959. On the show, the bowler who scored the most pins after three games was declared the winner and returned the next week to defend the title of King of the Hill. I won my first week and the next four weeks. I qualified for the show a few times after that but lost the TV competitions.

In 1966, the 1,500 members of the Merrimack Valley Bowling Association elected me their bowler of the year. I got a trophy, a beautiful blue velvet cape, and a crown decorated with red and blue stones. This is a part of my life I will always really cherish.

I continue to bowl to this day, but not in competition—only for pleasure.

LOUIS PALAZZO ◆ SALEM, NH

VINTAGE AD

1962

FRESH FROM MOTOROLA... new leader in the lively art of electronics

A STUNNING AD from the Fresh from Motorola print campaign that ran through the early 1960s featured electronics in ultracontemporary settings. Here, architect Leon Deller's subterranean rec room design has aquarium windows that look into the backyard pool. Look closely and you'll see the TV remote on the table to the man's left.

Motorola believes TV should look good even when it's off

MOTOROLA

Lucky number 13, Richard Earnhardt, won the spelling bee in 1942 by correctly spelling *sacrilegious*.

If Only We'd Had Spell Check

With televisions just gaining popularity, it's no wonder the word was a challenge.

ISABELLE "BETTY" PRESTO ◆ LAFAYETTE, NJ

Every year, my school held a spelling bee. Spelling was one of my best subjects, so of course I wanted to enter. The contest was for those of us in grades four through six.

This was 1936 and it was my first spelling bee. I was in fourth grade and I was competing against sixth-graders. After weeks of numerous rounds during the competition, I became very sure of myself—so sure that I spelled the words without giving them a second thought.

Well, believe it or not, the mistake I made was on a word that wasn't too popular back then. The word, in fact, is extremely popular now, but I spelled it really fast without thinking, like this: t-e-l-i-v-i-s-i-o-n. Can you imagine?

No one would make that mistake nowadays. Because of my error, I didn't win the contest and missed the trip to Washington, D.C.

I learned a hard lesson that day about being overconfident—one I'll never forget.

Museum Quality

His love for Star Wars came full circle when he met George Lucas.

JAMES CATALANO ◆ BERWYN, IL

A Jedi's ready for anything, even a game of pool! James' Obi-Wan Kenobi costume is a Halloween favorite. He also made this custom lightsaber (below) from a vintage Graflex flashbulb holder.

So many *Star Wars* memories! I was 12 when I first saw *Star Wars*. I was hooked.

I once had all the original Kenner action figures. If I had kept them, I'd have a gold mine, I'm sure. I held on to some of my *Star Wars* toys, but the collection isn't as big as it used to be. My first toy lightsaber had an inflatable blade. Years later I bought a $100 Force FX lightsaber, then made my own custom model from a vintage Graflex camera flash handle. *Star Wars* is the only movie series that I'd try to see at midnight showings. I'd dress in costume and have lightsaber battles with fellow fans.

My best *Star Wars* memories came at my job, when I worked at the Museum of Science and Industry in Chicago. In October 2007, the museum featured the traveling exhibit "*Star Wars*: Where Science Meets Imagination." It featured actual models, costumes and props from the *Star Wars* series. One was Luke Skywalker's landspeeder, another a full-size mock-up of the *Millennium Falcon*'s cockpit, where lucky visitors could experience a simulated jump to hyperspace. The museum's management even allowed employees to dress in character while working in the exhibit. I wore my Obi-Wan Kenobi costume.

The best moment of that exhibit was meeting George Lucas, who was doing media interviews. I'll never forget that.

Matthew and Rebecca King in the Halloween costumes their father, Richard, made in 1977.

Hollywood Halloween

During the summer of 1977, after my family saw *Star Wars*, we were all hooked on, if not slightly obsessed with, the movie. My dad, Richard, spent many evenings in the garage of our Riverside, Rhode Island, home that summer and fall making *Star Wars* Halloween costumes for us. My 9-year-old brother Matthew was C-3PO; I was 7 and dressed as R2-D2. I lobbied to wear roller skates so I could glide like R2-D2, but once I realized that one slip would put me on the ground, I gave up on the idea. We won every costume contest in town and were the hit of our neighborhood! On Halloween night, my dad cut a slit in the front of my costume and taped a paper bag inside so that candy could slip through.

I trot out this photograph on Halloween and when I trade *Star Wars* stories with others. People can't believe my dad made the costumes.

REBECCA KING ◆ CHARLESTOWN, MA

LONGING TO BE LAURA

CROWNED WITH A SUNBONNET, 12-year-old Donna Alice Patton won first place at her school's costume party wearing this Laura Ingalls-style dress in the late 1960s. Donna's mother made the outfit from her daughter's bedsheets, which were decorated with hearts and pink and red flowers. "I always wanted to be Laura," says Donna, who lives in Hillsboro, Ohio, and is a lifelong fan of the books. "Her life just seemed so much more interesting than my suburban world."

THE USUAL SUSPECTS

DURING A GAME OF CLUE, John Seiz of Highland Heights, Ohio, snapped his mother, Mary, sister Phyllis, father, Edwin, and brother George in a moment of deception in 1960.

BROTHERS ON BIKES

THE MORFIS BROTHERS, George, Teddy and Frank, pose in front of their father's dump trucks near their home in East Meadow, New York, in 1944. George, now of Ronkonkoma, New York, said his dad was a gunner's mate in the Merchant Marine. George and his brothers would ride their bikes to the bus stop to meet him whenever he got a weekend pass.

THE WOMEN in Jean Stafford's Winchester, Massachusetts, neighborhood gathered regularly at each other's houses for dinner and a few hands of bridge. They always dressed to the nines, says Jean's daughter Norma Jean Hissong of Olympia, Washington. This picture was taken in 1956.

MARBLES WAS OUR GAME

THE PLAYGROUND WAS THE PLACE to be every day before school started in the early 1940s. Dominick Sidoti of Washington, New Jersey, said his favorite game was school bells: Once the bell rang, the fellow who grabbed the most marbles won. Here, the gang ringing the circle consisted of (from left) Dominick, Donald, Henry, Tony and Jackie.

STEERING THE WHEEL

"MY CONSTANT DESIRE whenever we visited my grandparents in Elk County, Pennsylvania, was to drive the little car," says Joan Wheeler of Erie, Pennsylvania. "They rarely agreed, but on this sunny day in 1941, I finally got my wish." Joan sits at the wheel with her cousins and her big sister Mary (with glasses) standing by.

1949

A MERE SIX YEARS before Bill Haley's seminal hit, "Rock Around the Clock," this RCA ad seems to anticipate the always-on culture of rock 'n' roll, which was helped along by the portable radio.

1947

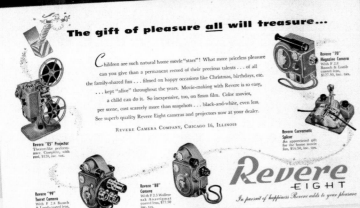

THE REVERE CAMERA CO. glorified the growing home-movie craze of the late '40s with a line of 8 mm cameras and supporting devices, such as a splicer for editing. "Color movies, per scene, cost scarcely more than snapshots," the ad says. But the equipment was pricey: The projector alone was $120, or about $1,350 today.

> " *My husband Mark and I were newlyweds in this photo. I had changed from my wedding dress into a three-piece hot pants outfit along with calf-high go-go boots.* "

BONNIE ABRAMS ◆ FORT PAYNE, AL

AT WORK

Whether it was just for a summer or the beginning of a career, every job had a way of teaching valuable lessons.

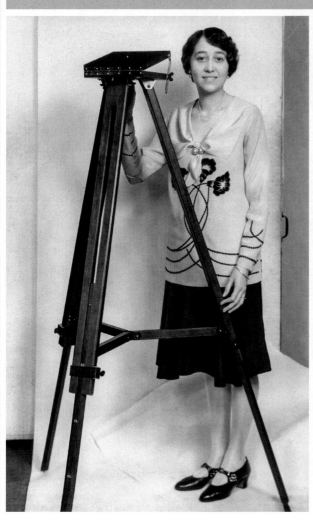

CHAPTER 5

Journey Through Space

During the space race, photos and miniature models stirred our imaginations.

ORSON C. HAYNIE ◆ PORTLAND, OR

This prototype of the space shuttle was built for engineering purposes in the Rockwell model shop.

Orson and two co-workers make final adjustments on the display he created for the 1975 Paris Air Show.

In a concept drawing from about 1977 (left), a space shuttle, with cargo bay doors open and retrieving arm extended, launches an early Global Positioning System (GPS) satellite into space.

The summer of 1966, after my sophomore year of college, I worked for North American Aviation, an aerospace technology company. I worked in the publications and promotions division at its headquarters in El Segundo, California.

NAA was one of the prime contractors on the Apollo lunar landing program, so it was an exciting time to work there. The race was on to beat the Russians to the moon. The company merged with Rockwell Standard in 1967 and became North American Rockwell. Rockwell built the Apollo command and service modules, the second stage on the Saturn V rocket, and the ascent engine on the lunar module.

One man at NAA, Tugrul Uke, took me under his wing and taught me much about the business. I worked there for three summers while attending college and studying advertising, speech and graphic arts. Tugrul trained me in external publications, photography, movie production and trade show exhibits.

During my second summer at NAA, I put together an audiovisual presentation to document and showcase the workings of the Saturn V rocket. I showed it at schools, churches and Scout organizations. NAA liked the idea so much that it arranged for me to show the presentation at other companies and organizations.

After graduating from college in 1970, I was hired full time and moved to Pittsburgh, Pennsylvania, where I continued my audiovisual exhibit work until 1977.

Over the years, I've updated my presentation with images and information about NASA Skylab, the first American manned space station; the Apollo-Soyuz mission; and the Hubble Space Telescope. I'm still showing it 45 years later.

My truly amazing journey included meeting Jim Irwin of Apollo 15 and Wally Schirra of Mercury, Gemini and Apollo fame.

Sure, I Can Do That!

He volunteered on a whim but gained a better job and a friendship.

MIKE CALL ◆ SPARKS, NV

Grass Valley, California, the town where I was born in 1938, was the heart of hard rock, or lode, mining along the Gold Rush trail. When I was a teen, my father told me stories about many of the mines that operated there before World War II, including the New Brunswick, the North Star and the Empire.

During hard times in 1936, my father headed to the New Brunswick mine to look for work. There were about 30 men standing outside the superintendent's shack with the same idea. When the superintendent came out on the deck, he announced that he needed a powder man. Looking around, my dad noticed that no one was raising a hand. He immediately raised his and announced that he was a powder man.

The mine superintendent looked at my dad and said, "Here's Red, your driller. Follow him to the mine shack, change into your work clothes, and get a hat and carbide lantern."

As my dad and his new crew member walked to the shack, Red said, "You've never popped a cap in your life, have you?"

"No!" my dad answered. "But I need a job real bad."

Red told him not to worry; he used to blast but had switched to drilling because it paid more. "I'll teach you everything you need to know," Red said, "and we'll get along fine."

They became best friends and worked together for four years. When World War II came along, all precious metal mines closed and resources such as dynamite, steel drills and fuel were redirected to the war effort.

Some 100 men working the New Brunswick mine in June 1938 gathered outside the pits.

1888
Inventor George Eastman coins the word "Kodak," introduces the Kodak box camera with its self-contained roll of film, and launches what would become an industry standard.

1892
The business, started in 1880, is now known as the Eastman Kodak Co.

1900
Kodak launches the Brownie camera. It sells for $1; film is 15 cents a roll.

1935
Kodachrome becomes the first color film available for hobbyists.

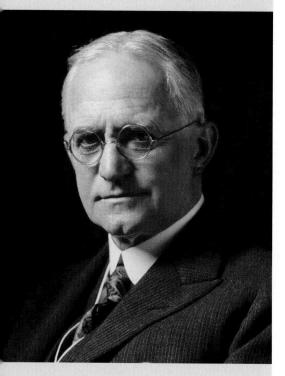

Oughta Be in Pictures

With a knack for experimentation, she developed a career in film and portrait photography.

VIRGINIA PAGE ◆ DEERFIELD BEACH, FL

My mom, Emily Frech Ballard, was the oldest child of German immigrants in the early 1900s. By the time she was in her teens, America was fighting Germany in World War I, and anti-German sentiment had grown in the U.S. As a result, her father lost his job. The family of six had no income, so Mom left high school to work as a package wrapper at Marshall Field's department store.

One day while my mom was at the department store, a supervisor with the Bell System in Chicago asked if she would like a job as a phone operator at its main office. At age 17, this was her lucky break. In her role at Bell, Mom developed a novel pattern of relaying long-distance calls. Her ingenuity led to her moving to another office that needed someone to photograph employees for their identification badges.

Emily's tripod, made of wood and metal, was sturdy enough to accommodate large cameras.

She went to photography school in Michigan with one other woman and six men—among them, Allen Funt of *Candid Camera* fame. When she returned to work, she was put in charge of all ID badges. While taking photos for Western Electric, a part of the Bell System, she met my dad.

In the meantime, Universal asked Kodak to find technicians to work on Technicolor prints, a new process for colorizing film. When it contacted Bell, my mom's boss recommended her, based on the developing techniques she was already using.

My family still has many of the early color photos. Each image took hours to develop. The color in them appeared to blend together and the contrast was not as sharp as in today's.

Best of all, working on this huge project gave my mom enough money to open her own portrait studio in the Chicago area.

GEORGE EASTMAN: AP/SHUTTERSTOCK

Skating Marvels

Because I enjoyed roller-skating so much, I took my skates with me when I went into the military service. When I got home, I skated at the Rollaire skating rink in Manitowoc, Wisconsin, where several of us started doing acts during intermission.

In 1947, Bob VanHaren, my cousin's husband, was performing as an acrobat with the Billy Schultz Indoor Circus of Manitowoc. He invited me to visit after work to perfect my skating.

Ed Keiper was also with the circus and managed the Rollaire rink. Soon I was skating with Ed and his girlfriend, Rosemary Pyne, as The Skating Marvels. We performed all over the state. It was great fun. Our largest audience—more than 6,000 people— was at a Fourth of July celebration.

I met my future wife, Jeannette, at one of our performances. We were married on Nov. 27, 1948. Soon skating with my children replaced professional skating. I am 88 years old and cherish my memories of those days in the circus.

EARL JUNK ◆ MANITOWOC, WI

The roller-skating trio (above)—from left, Ed Keiper, Rosemary Pyne and Earl Junk—toured with the Billy Schultz Indoor Circus, started by performer-instructor Billy Schultz. Here, Earl spins Ed and Rosemary in one of their roller-skating routines.

Testing the Sky's Limits

His uncle wasn't afraid to step in, and in the process helped shape history.

MARK W. JOHNSON • VALRICO, FL

My late uncle Deane Cunningham was one of several pilots who developed and certified the B-29 Superfortress, the Boeing aircraft that transported and dropped the atomic bombs on Hiroshima and Nagasaki.

Born in Phillips, Maine, in 1902, Deane learned to fly Standard D.1 biplanes at a once-popular airport in Kewanee, Illinois, that is now a shopping center. His aviation exploits as a professional pilot included airmail, stunt flying and charter businesses. His advanced flight training was conducted in 1925 at Burdette Field in Los Angeles, California. His instructor was the colorful pilot Jack Frye, who years later became president of Trans World Airlines.

When hostilities broke out in Europe and Germany invaded Poland in 1939, Deane left the United States for service with the Royal Canadian Air Force. When his four years of service ended, he returned to the U.S. as a qualified multiengine-aircraft test pilot.

Around that time, Boeing was looking for test pilots with Deane's specific skill set. The company's latest long-range bomber, the B-29, was proving to be a challenge. The new bomber

Always impeccably dressed, Deane carried himself with a deliberate step. His confidence, flying experience and calm demeanor influenced his nephew Mark, who went on to become an airline captain many years later.

suffered numerous setbacks including fuel leaks, electrical problems and uncontained fires.

Test pilot Eddie Allen and his crew died when the XB-29 prototype caught fire in flight and crashed, killing all crew members and 20 factory workers on the ground, and instigating a mass exodus of many remaining crews. With time a critical factor, Deane was hired and completed test-flight operations until the aircraft was fully operational.

After that point, Col. Paul Tibbets and the crew of the *Enola Gay* attained fame when the first atomic bomb, Little Boy, was dropped on Hiroshima, Japan, on Aug. 6, 1945. Days later Japan sought to surrender when a second bomb dropped by a B-29 named *Bockscar* decimated Nagasaki.

Although Uncle Deane never sought notoriety, his aviation experiences spanned the entire spectrum of powered flight over a 35-year period. He flew everything from fabric-covered biplanes built during the golden age of aviation to the first swept-wing supersonic strategic jet bomber, the B-47.

Deane was the oldest jet test pilot at Boeing when he died suddenly in 1955 at the age of 52. He left behind his wife, my aunt Mona Wallingford Cunningham.

From Grandma's Garden to the Sport of Kings

MARTHA CRAWFORD CANTARINI ◆ DENMAN ISLAND, BC

Henry Ford had nothing on my grandmother. She had her own production line with her three children in her vegetable garden in Durant, Oklahoma, in 1914. Grandmother hoed the soil, the oldest poked the hole, the next boy dropped in the seeds, and my mother, Sharon Crawford, took up the rear, patting the soil down.

My mother was a special breed. After getting kicked out of her high school for smoking, she ran away to Dallas and launched her dream of becoming somebody. At 17, she became a model for Neiman Marcus in 1925. She was especially beautiful and was asked to drive a new automobile in a local parade dressed as a Spanish senorita. That's where she met my father, Charles F. McKee. He died when I was 6 months old.

In 1930, my mother met a dashing professional polo player, Carl Crawford, on the Texas Special train out of St. Louis. They were married two years later.

My mother's startling beauty eventually led to a screen test at Paramount Studios. But, unfortunately, she photographed a lot like Claudette Colbert, which didn't sit well with the movie star. My mother's film career was unofficially over before it began.

Instead, she decided to pour her energy into working with Carl, who managed several polo clubs all the way from Chicago to California. She also became an official timer for the U.S. Polo Association.

By 1939, polo was in full swing in California, and she got to welcome big stars such as Walt Disney and Spencer Tracy, along with famed directors, producers and writers, to the various clubs Carl managed.

My mother's promotion from third in the garden production line in Oklahoma to the toast of the Hollywood polo set seems like a dream—but it's all true.

Sharon Crawford at 6 in her mother's garden (below) in Durant, Oklahoma, around 1914. At right, Sharon, center, laughs with Hollywood luminaries, including Walt Disney, third from right, at the Uplifters Polo Club in Pacific Palisades, California, in 1939.

A Lot of Living in 39 Years

Dauntless in his pursuit of passion, one man moves beyond his past. **BILL G. KING** ◆ BIRMINGHAM, AL

During my early years in Huntsville, Alabama, I was part of a poor family. We lived in a boardinghouse at the Dallas Cotton Mill Village. I begged for pennies on the streets. At the age of 11, unable to live with my stepfather, I moved in with a bootlegger named Kathrin until I was 17. She treated me like a mother, and I loved her for it.

I lived many lives after that, including four years in the Air Force, where I was honored with three awards. I worked my way through Tennessee Technological University in Cookeville, Tennessee, laying sewer lines full time on campus to pay my college expenses before getting my bachelor's degree.

After college I went into real estate, where I developed, owned and operated 16 hotels/motels and 11 apartment complexes. In addition to my business activities and because of my relationships in the business community, I became interested in politics. I served in the Alabama House of Representatives and the Alabama Senate. It was there that I was chosen to direct Jimmy Carter's successful U.S. presidential campaign in Alabama.

Although I enjoyed business and politics, I also pursued other more physical activities such as skydiving, bungee jumping, scuba diving, paraplane flying and motorcycle racing.

Sitting on that pony 39 years earlier (below), I would never have believed that I would one day stand in the Oval Office of the White House and receive a national appointment from the president of the United States.

My experience is proof that a poor beginning should never be an excuse to slow you down.

President Jimmy Carter appointed Bill to the United States Advisory Commission on Intergovernmental Relations in 1978 (left). Bill was 5 in 1939 when his mom borrowed a dime to get her son's picture taken with a horse (below).

He Was a Pin and Ball Wizard

Beware of flying bowling balls!

MICHAEL L. MULLENIX ◆ CONVERSE, IN

During my sophomore and junior years of high school in the late 1950s, I found work as a pin boy at the Marion Bowlaire in Marion, Indiana.

Spotting pins was semi-automatic. Each lane had a rack with slots for each pin's position. When the ball hit the pins, we jumped into the pit, retrieved the ball and set it on the ball return, then grabbed the knocked-over pins and set them in the rack.

Errant pins rammed me in the shins a few times, and once I got a concussion when I was hit in the head. If a bowler threw exceptionally hard, smacking us with flying pins, we'd show our displeasure by putting a backspin on the ball in the return, so it wouldn't quite make it up at the other end. The bowler would have to chase his ball back down the lane. Revenge was sweet.

We'd pick up two pins in each hand while setting. Doing that day after day gave us forearms the size of Popeye's. No one would arm-wrestle us.

HE DELIVERS

MY GRANDFATHER Harrison Fairbanks was born in 1897, placed in an orphanage at age 6 and indentured to a single woman to work her farm. He ran away when he was 16 to reunite with his siblings in their hometown of Bradford, Pennsylvania.

When he finished high school, Harry got a job at a haberdashery 20 miles away in Olean, New York. While at work, he saw Nellie Rose walking down the street and decided to find out who she was. Nellie was going to nursing school at the time, but when she met Harry the two fell in love and married in 1917.

Six years later, in 1923, Harry found work as a rural letter carrier in nearby Portville, New York. He and Grandma delivered mail with their horse, Old Toots. Sometimes Grandma would meet Grandpa with the car for lunch and he would use the car to finish his deliveries.

My mom, Jean, would tell us about her dad bringing the mail home and the family separating it on the dining room table.

Once, a customer on his route put a cat in the mailbox. When Grandpa opened the flap, the cat jumped out of the mailbox, into the mail truck and out the other side. It was a good thing he had his door open.

During the war, if a letter came from a service member, Grandpa would deliver it right away, even if it was late or on a Sunday afternoon.

After 34 years on the job, Harry wanted the postmaster job in Portville. He and Nellie drove to Washington, D.C., to discuss the position with their representative.

Harry walked into the man's office, introduced himself and requested an interview. He was appointed postmaster in March 1958. Eventually he became the president of the Cattaraugus County Postmasters Association.

YVONNE BROWN ◆ YUCAIPA, CA

To Build Lightning in a Factory

She delivered the right parts to get the job done. **ETHEL KING MILLAR** • OCEANO, CA

We were at war in 1942 when I graduated from Burbank High School in California. So instead of going to college, I went to work as an expediter at Lockheed Aircraft Corp. near the airport in Burbank, where P-38 Lightning fighters and other warplanes were assembled.

Here's how the job worked: Every morning I received a list of parts needed on the assembly line. My job was to find the parts and deliver them where needed. The parts were in either of two plants. To get between locations, I rode a bicycle with a large basket. Sometimes the basket was so heavy, someone had to hold the bike as I got on, and give me a push to get started. I don't recall how I stopped.

If I couldn't find parts, I asked the buyer to order them. I bugged him until the parts came in, got them inspected and delivered them. It was quite the important job, especially for an 18-year-old. I was my own boss.

Ethel's co-worker entered her photo into Lockheed's Miss P-38 contest. She didn't win.

When I walked through the plants, I heard lots of whistles from the work crew, which I ignored, of course.

When I walked through the plants, I heard lots of whistles from the work crew, which I ignored, of course. But once, I stopped to give one of the men a big hug. When his fellow workers asked him how he rated such attention, he replied, "I married her sister." The crew member was my brother-in-law Rex Welker, who soon joined the Navy.

I met Lloyd Millar at the plant just before he entered the Air Force. We married when the war was over.

While I worked for Lockheed, the company held a competition to find someone to help with public relations photos. There were 38 contestants. I didn't win, but it was a thrill having my entry picture taken as I stood on the wing of a P-38. Although I usually wore a pantsuit to work (no jeans), I knew when my picture would be taken, so I brought my favorite dress that day to change into.

I am now a happy and healthy 92-year-old, and I wonder if any of the other contestants are still alive!

Fast Times at College Mall

During Melissa's shoe stint, Russ was one of her managers. He wore his sales pitch well.

Anytime I watch the movie *Fast Times at Ridgemont High* (1982), I am taken back to my years at the College Mall in Bloomington, Indiana. The movie depicts the life of a teenage mall worker to a T. I know because I worked in the mall.

The first phase of the College Mall opened in 1965, just a few days after I was born. I never really paid much attention to the old part of the mall.

But in 1982, the mall expanded, adding a new wing. I was a junior in high school and so excited about having a new hip side to the mall. Not only did I want to hang out there, I wanted to work there, too.

I spent three hours one afternoon going from store to store. Finally, I came to the Thom McAn shoe store. It was a slow day for shoe sales, so Wayne Beckes, the manager, interviewed me on the spot. I was thrilled when he offered me a job.

I started in December 1982 and worked there 4½ years, until June 1987.

I became quite the skilled salesperson. One sales technique I would use involved going out to the benches in front of the store to demonstrate the store's leather shoe cleaner to men waiting for their wives. I'd start by cleaning one shoe for one man. He would love the look of that clean shoe and then ask me to do the other.

I would tell him that I'd gladly clean the other shoe if he bought our great cleaning product. I sold lots of that shoe cleaner using that technique.

I still think of those years at Thom McAn as some of my best. Selling shoes in a mall with 12 other shoe stores nearby was quite a challenge, but it prepared me for so many other challenges I would face later in life. And just like Stacy in the movie, I had a big crush on a salesman at the nearby RadioShack.

MELISSA PATE ◆ SOLSBERRY, IN

WHAT CAME FIRST, THE CHICKEN OR...

MY PATH to becoming a butcher was a bit unassuming. I was 16, in high school and in need of a part-time job.

There was a market near our home, so I thought I'd start there.

The owner, Mr. Hale, was very kind and asked me only one question: "Can you draw a chicken?"

I was no artist, but I badly needed the job, so I said yes.

How was I to know that what he actually meant was to clean a chicken with its head and feet on?!

I reported to the market the next afternoon at 4. They gave me a white apron and a knife, showed me a pile of chickens and told me to get to work. This was not at all what I thought I'd be doing. Fortunately, another employee showed me the ropes.

That first job got me into the meat-cutting business. After working for many grocery stores for 46 years, I retired. And I definitely still know how to draw a chicken.

JOHN A. HALBERT
VANCOUVER, WA

In his butcher coat, tie optional, John Halbert wears the standard uniform of his profession.

PUT A MOVE ON

TAKEN IN TIJUANA, MEXICO, in 1916, this photo shows a moving business using draft horses. Joan K. Hunt of Lebanon, Oregon, said her great-grandfather J. Ad Johnson ran the company based in San Ysidro, California.

SPECIAL DELIVERY

"MY FAMILY lived in defense housing near Hickham Field and Pearl Harbor," says James E. Page, now of Lady Lake, Florida. "After the attack, I delivered newspapers while carrying a gas mask over my shoulder."

STOCKING UP

GLADYS AND CHARLES E. RHODES owned this grocery store on Watts Hill in Charleston, West Virginia, in the mid-1930s. Their son Charles, of Placerville, California, said people would call in orders and a crew would deliver them in Chevy panel trucks.

TEENAGE DRIVER

AT AGE 18, Francis Willis "Monte" Montague, far left, was one of the few people with Brig. Gen. John J. Pershing who could drive a White Motor Co. truck, so he was made a driver for the U.S. Army's 5th Motor Transport Company. Monte's grandson Thomas V. Johnson, of Anacortes, Washington, sent the photo, taken in New Mexico in 1916.

LOOKING DAPPER

SHOWING OFF THE DAILY SPECIALS, Michael Yurovich, 19, poses during a stop along the delivery route for Essex Bakery in Lorain, Ohio. Michael's son Daniel of Vermilion, shared this picture taken in 1930.

PROTECTORS OF THE CROSSING

TEACHER VIRGINIA THURTLE took this picture of crossing guards at her Euclid, Ohio, school in the 1950s. Virginia's niece Mary V. Palmer sent the photo.

Tough Work in the Tropics

Dressed in protective gear, I learned to take down a pineapple in one swift move. **KEN BUSH** ◆ NORTHFIELD, VT

As a picker, Ken snacked on pineapples that entire summer. He ate so many pineapples as a teenager that he now avoids them.

No summer job was harder or more adventurous than the one I had in 1972, when I was 17. My two best friends and I were recruited to pick fruit for Dole through our Boy Scout troop in Idaho Falls, Idaho. Since the only summer job in our area was moving irrigation pipe in potato fields, pineapple picking on the island of Lanai sounded more exotic, not to mention far from home.

Dole hired us for $1.60 an hour and we were issued state of Hawaii work permits. The company chartered a flight from Salt Lake City, Utah, to Honolulu. It also promised to pay the return flight for each picker who successfully completed the entire commitment. Those who went home early for anything other than a medical reason would have to pay their own way.

Strict standards of decorum were expected of each picker hired. There was no dating of island girls, no tobacco or alcohol use, no gambling and no fighting.

Because Hawaiian resident workers had the day shift, our group was assigned the swing shift, 2:30 p.m. to 11 p.m. That left mornings free for us to hit the beach, a treat most Idaho boys had never experienced. We learned to snorkel and body surf. Some of us bought surfboards and took them back on the return flight.

Before heading to the fields, we were taught how to properly pick the fruit: too green and it wouldn't ripen,

too yellow and it would be good only for juice or canning. It was our responsibility to judge whether each pineapple was ready.

Dressing for work took some effort. Because pineapple plant leaves have sharp spurs, we donned heavy denim pants covered with thick cotton chaps. To protect our arms, we wore long-sleeved shirts with denim arm protectors. We had wire-mesh eye protectors with an elastic cinch band that tightened behind the head. A brimmed hat, leather gloves and laced work boots completed the uniform.

Every afternoon a fleet of large open-top trucks would transport us to the fields. These same trucks would haul the newly picked pineapples back as well.

The picking technique took a bit of practice. We grasped the short, spiny fruit top and, with a twist, the pineapple would pop off the plant. Still holding the top, we would snap the pineapple to detach it from its top. Voilà! Both parts hit the belt.

I grossed $800 for the entire summer but brought home only half that after I paid Dole for room and board. That was the toughest $400 I've ever earned.

Ken was caked in Hawaiian red dirt by the end of his pineapple-picking shift.

PINEAPPLE: MALGORZATA LITKOWSKA/SHUTTERSTOCK

Best Summer Job Ever

You didn't have to look far to find fun. **PAUL ROMANIELLO** ◆ DANBURY, CT

Yes, that was me, a lifeguard. It was the summer of 1959, I was 18 and I'd just been hired at a private beach in Darien, Connecticut. It was a small beach with a pier and a swim platform for jumping or diving. The beach was used exclusively by the residents of the 60 or so homes in the immediate area.

There was nothing to the job. All I had to do was sit in the sun and watch for swimmers in distress. I had absolutely no certification to be a lifeguard, but I at least was a good swimmer. Two fellow lifeguards and I rotated positions during the day: We'd spend one hour on the beach, one hour on the pier and one hour at the food shack selling snacks.

When it rained, the lifeguards would resort to doing routine maintenance or retreating inside the food shack to play chess or other board games. The time we spent playing those games helped solidify friendships that ended up lasting for years.

In the evening, we regrouped with other teens who had regular jobs as well. Then the nighttime ritual began. We either coaxed someone to drive us to the Tastee Freez or convinced the owner of the car with the biggest trunk to head to a drive-in movie. The third option was to just hang around and shoot the breeze.

If things worked out, some of the guys and gals paired up with their No. 1 squeezes and commandeered vehicles for the sole purpose of what we called "watching the submarine races" from the water's edge.

The cast of characters would change periodically throughout the summer, but the routine was more or less the same. I may not have made much money, but when you're 18, that's not a major consideration.

Just hanging out at the beach was the perfect way to spend a summer, according to Paul.

The Long, Hot Summer

In Miami heat, I steamed through my first teaching job.

KEN McCULLOUGH ◆ WALLAND, TN

After I graduated with my teaching certification in June 1962, I was hired to teach American history and English at Miami Norland Senior High School in Miami, Florida. My new contract wouldn't start until the fall, which meant I'd have to keep working as a ticket agent for Eastern Air Lines, one of several jobs I'd taken to get myself through school. I was eager to start teaching, but I couldn't afford to do nothing over the summer. So I was delighted when I was asked to teach summer school at Miami Jackson Senior High School.

Jackson was in a large district, Allapattah, and the school building stretched several blocks along 36th Street, the main artery to the airport. With no air conditioning, we ventilated it the old-fashioned way, by keeping windows open.

I knew it was going to be a hard summer when I got a classroom with large windows facing 36th Street. They rattled with the rumble of every truck and car that passed by. On top of that, directly across the street was a radio repair shop with a loudspeaker on the sidewalk blaring tunes from a local station.

Endurance was the only option. I loosened my tie and waited for my students.

I was to be the overflow social studies teacher, meaning I'd get spillover students from any overenrolled class. I thought they'd be from the same class, but no. Several ninth-graders from a civics class walked in. Then came some 10th-grade world history students. Then a few 12th-grade U.S. government students. Then more 10th-graders. By midmorning, I had a class of 40 in three grade levels. It was hot and, with the music next door, the 36th Street traffic and the kids talking, very, very noisy.

Nothing at college had prepared me for this. I decided to just level with the students.

"I can't stop the guy from playing his radio," I told them. "I can't stop the trucks from going by or their horns from blowing, but I'm going to work and you will, too. We are in this together."

There was a lot going on that summer—problems with Russia, fears of nuclear war, talk of space exploration, conflicts in Southeast Asia and North Africa, battles over civil rights. I often started with a group talk about current events before breaking into grade levels. It was a grind during the hottest season in Miami, but I don't recall a single student failing.

I think often about those six weeks, and I hope the students do, too. It turned out we had a good time, music, heat, noise and all.

> *Nothing at college had prepared me for this. I decided to just level with the students.*

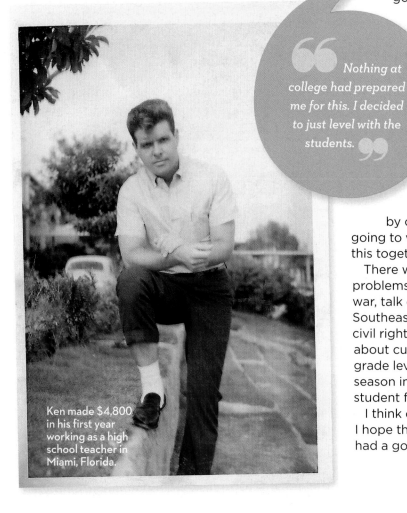

Ken made $4,800 in his first year working as a high school teacher in Miami, Florida.

"*During my career in the Army in the late 1950s, I was stationed at a barracks outside Kaiserslautern, Germany. One day on guard duty, I was assigned to the motor pool gate and had to turn away a civilian Oldsmobile sedan and send it to the main gate, even though a lieutenant in the car was cross with me.*"

BENNETT YOUNG ◆ ORCHARD PARK, NY

WE FOUGHT THE WARS TOGETHER

Everyone stepped up when it mattered most. Read on for tales of courage, bravery and personal sacrifice during challenging periods in our history.

CHAPTER 6

The military's strict guidelines about appearance applied to the Women's Army Air Corps during WWII when Ruth served. Uniforms included wool olive drab for winter service and khaki cotton, shown here, for summer service.

Women in Uniform

My mother, Ruth Morgan, was a part of the Women's Army Air Corps near Portland, Oregon, where she met and married her husband. Years later, her grandson's wife, Laci Gausnell (near right), modeled the olive green WWII uniform and garrison cap. The best part of having her uniform is sharing it with my children, grandchildren and great-grandchildren.

PATRICIA GAUSNELL ◆ ROSEBURG, OR

Ruth (far right) served in the honor guard when President Harry Truman visited her base.

The Day His World Changed

Stationed in Hawaii, he was there for the day that lives in infamy.

JACK DOYLE ◆ TAYLORVILLE, IL

The scene that Sunday was familiar. Newspapers announced 15 shopping days until Christmas. Business was good, thanks to lend-lease, a law passed in 1941 that established the principal means for providing U.S. military aid to foreign nations during the early stages of WWII. Negotiations with the Japanese were at a standstill. Jukeboxes played "Boogie Woogie Bugle Boy," "New San Antonio Rose" and "Walking the Floor Over You."

The sun rose gloriously over the islands, and Dec. 7 would have been a wonderful time to explore Oahu, go into Honolulu or stay aboard ship and write letters to loved ones. I was 21, in the service two years, and I personally planned to stay aboard ship for a day of rest and relaxation.

About 0740 hours, I stood alone portside on the deck of the USS *Tennessee*, next to the USS *West Virginia*, looking over the shipyard that serviced U.S. Navy vessels. The battleships of the Pacific Fleet—the *California*, the *Maryland*, the *Oklahoma*, the *Tennessee*, the *West Virginia*, the *Arizona* and the *Nevada*—lay anchored alongside Ford Island. USS *Pennsylvania* was in dry dock, and the rest of the harbor was spotted with cruisers, destroyers and ships of every size—a display of the greatest sea power in the world.

As I thought about my parents and siblings, I watched a force of fighters, dive bombers and torpedo planes arrive over the Koolau Mountain Range. The planes flew low enough and close enough that I could plainly see the pilots' faces and their fur-collared jackets with white scarves. They passed the *Arizona*, the *West Virginia*, the *Oklahoma* and the *Maryland*. I counted 10, 20, 30, 40 of them. Although I saw the red ball painted on the wings, I still did not realize they were Japanese.

Suddenly I heard a loud explosion and saw dirt and smoke rising in the sky ahead and to the right of my ship. Only then did I realize we were under attack. I was witnessing the first minute of the official entry of the United States into World War II. The planes had flown to the airfields, destroying our planes and hangars before returning to bomb the battleships.

In the mayhem, I heard these orders: "All hands, man your battle station. This is no drill." I heard that message many times in the months to follow, but that first time will live with me forever.

> " All hands, man your battle station. This is no drill. "

Crewmates Lindsey, Kearse and Jack Doyle spent carefree days aboard ship before the Japanese attacked.

'Guess Where I Am'

It was a typical winter Sunday in Paterson, New Jersey—bleak with just enough wind blowing to make it uncomfortably cold as we left 10 a.m. Mass at St. Joseph Church.

"Want to play some basketball?" Chicksie Clegg asked a group of us standing in front of the church, hunched over and shivering against the cold. We agreed it was something to do. We borrowed the key to the gym from the nuns at the convent and played until boredom set in.

As we headed home, one of the boys shouted, "Hey, I shouldn't have to go to school tomorrow. Today's December 7th and my birthday is on the 8th. So wish me a happy birthday."

When I reached home on East 23rd Street, I walked across the front porch, glancing into the window where my uncles and aunt lived, and was mildly surprised to find no one in the living room.

On Sundays, Uncles Joe, Frank and John usually sat there reading the Sunday papers.

After my father's death, my mother, my aunt and I lived on the second floor. I raced upstairs and discovered the whole family in a semicircle in the living room. They were leaning forward and intensely focused on the family-sized radio. Uncle John was still in his Sunday-go-to-Mass suit, while Uncle Joe was in his uniform, ready to go on his highway patrol route.

Something had their attention. My mother put her finger to her lips, signaling me to keep silent. Although the New York Giants and Brooklyn Dodgers were playing the final game of the season, I couldn't imagine this grabbing such attention—especially from my aunt and mother. During a break, my mother whispered, "The Japanese have bombed Pearl Harbor."

Brought to shore by amphibious landing craft, U.S. infantrymen wade onto Omaha Beach during the D-Day invasion on June 6, 1944.

"Where's Pearl Harbor?" I asked.

"I think it's off the coast of Alaska," Uncle Joe said.

The radio newsman soon guided us to its location "in the American territory of Hawaii."

"This means we'll be at war with Japan," Uncle John proclaimed, adding, "At least it won't involve Jackie." He based his prediction on my age—15 at the time.

The family meeting soon broke up, and the evening meal was particularly silent.

Fast forward to June 1944. I was crouched in the Navy landing craft, waiting for it to scrape the beach and its heavy ramp to fall open and hit the ground so I could wade ashore as a 17-year-old Navy petty officer assigned to the 2nd Naval Beach Battalion on Utah Beach, Normandy.

I couldn't help but think of my uncle's earlier prediction. If I'd had a cellphone back then, I would have called him and asked, "Can you guess where I am, Uncle John?"

JACK RASKOPF ◆ FORT WORTH, TX

A MODEST OVERSIGHT

EVERYONE who went through basic military training had a humiliating moment the first time back home. Usually it was about using bad language at the table. Mine was a bit different.

I was used to living with 59 other men. The first thing we'd do when entering the barracks was remove our boots so we wouldn't get black marks all over the floor. Then we would take off our clothes.

My first day back home, I was getting ready to take a shower when my sister asked me what I was doing. So I told her.

"Do you always get undressed in front of people?" she asked.

That's when I realized I was standing in the living room in front of my sister and three of her friends, wearing nothing but my underwear.

EDWARD J. "JACK" DECKERD
PERRYVILLE, MO

A view of Battleship Row after the bombings shows the USS *Arizona* in the center, sunken and burning. To the left are the USS *Tennessee* and USS *West Virginia*, which later became seaworthy after repair.

A Ship and Its Crew Remembered

Years later, a father reflected on surviving a sinking ship at Pearl Harbor.

CAROL KITANO ◆ BURIEN, WA

My father, William E. Clothier, was a 20-year-old Marine private aboard the battleship USS *Nevada* when Japanese torpedo planes and dive bombers attacked Pearl Harbor on Dec. 7, 1941. Although he recently died, he was interviewed many times about his experience.

He recalled that fateful Sunday with a cold feeling in his stomach.

My father said the day was bright and beautiful just before 8 a.m. when he and a friend were dressing for church. That's when they heard gunfire. "We had been undergoing several alerts, and we were sure that it was someone playing with the guns," he explained.

Even after an officer came through the ship yelling "General quarters! We are being attacked!" he and his friend still thought it was part of a practice session.

My father was on Gun 10, and when he ran into the gun casemate he saw a plane go down in flames right in front of him. His first thought was that this was the most realistic drill he had ever seen. Then a burst of bullets ricocheted off the side of the casemate, and it became clear that this was no drill.

"We were hit again and again, and the ship started to sink," he said. "A Marine gunnery chief in the station opposite mine had his clothes torn off him, and three men were killed by a blast. The chief raced onto the boat deck and grabbed a machine gun and kept on fighting. He was cited with the Navy Cross for his action."

The bombed *Nevada* was sinking rapidly in the channel and would have blocked the path to all boats if tugs had not pushed the battleship to the beach. With the ship already partially submerged, men kept firing their guns. Others brought ammunition to the gun stations, holding the bullets over their heads to keep them out of the water.

The captain's boat had been overturned, and he waded through oil-slicked water to reach the *Nevada*. His first remarks upon reaching deck were "My God! My God! What have they done to my boys?"

My father didn't talk much about his experiences until 1985, when he attended his first reunion of Pearl Harbor veterans. This awakened a new interest in the battle and the history of his ship.

The *Nevada* earned a total of seven battle stars and was the only battleship present at both Pearl Harbor and the Normandy landings.

His first thought was that this was the most realistic drill he had ever seen.

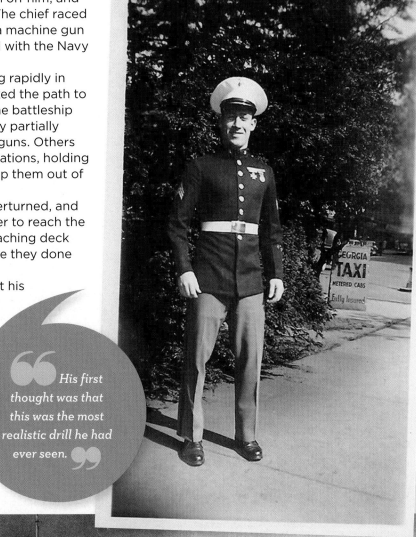

Staff Sgt. William E. Clothier, U.S. Marines, poses in uniform (above). Shown here, the USS *Nevada* sat beached and burning after the Japanese attack. The *Nevada* was the only battleship from Pearl Harbor sent to participate in the Normandy invasion on D-Day.

Triumph of the American Dream

Our father, Gilbert Hinchcliffe, was born in Liverpool, England, in 1904. When he was 16, he came to America by himself with only $15 in his pocket. After a tiresome delay at Ellis Island, he landed on the docks in New York City and searched for work. He held menial jobs aboard different ships to support himself, then joined the Merchant Marine and rose to the rank of chief engineer. He became a naturalized citizen in 1929, when he was 24.

In 1938, he met Melva, the woman who would become his wife and our mother. She was a physical therapy student at what was then Walter Reed General Hospital in Washington, D.C. When America entered World War II, Dad joined the Coast Guard, where he served as an officer for 24 years and retired as a captain in 1966. He was captain of the port—the officer with broad authority over port protection and enforcement—in Savannah, Georgia, from 1957 to 1961.

Mom and Dad had four children: Carol, Jean, Marcia and Stephen. Dad was a fine and honorable man who truly lived the American dream. He started with nothing and served his family and adopted country well. A hero to his family, he passed away in Savannah in 1992.

JEAN H. McRAE ◆ SAVANNAH, GA

Capt. Gilbert Hinchcliffe (top left) poses during his years in Georgia. In 1946, Melva and Gilbert Hinchcliffe (top photo) lived in Baltimore, Maryland, while he served in the Coast Guard at Sparrows Point. Rear Adm. Willard Smith (bottom photo) honors Gilbert with a medal for distinguished service at his retirement in 1966.

Those Big Blue Eyes

This Marine's wife found that it pays to know people in high places. **WILLIAM C. SMITH** ◆ CINCINNATI, OH

Still together, Bill and Alice spent the first year of marriage at Marine bases from the East Coast to the West.

People said we were too young, but my high school sweetheart, Alice, and I were married at the end of our senior year in May 1944. I had enlisted in the Marine Corps the month before and was called for active duty in August. I spent my time in basic training on Parris Island, South Carolina, before being sent to Camp Lejeune, North Carolina.

About a week after I arrived, Alice showed up and rented a cabin across from the base. The place was really just a shack with a coal oil heater and cracks in the roof so big you could see planes fly over. When it rained, we used buckets.

Alice became friends with the woman next door, who was married to a sergeant on base. One day the friend told Alice the Marines were sending 100 troops to sea school in San Diego but one had dropped out for medical reasons.

Alice begged me to ask the sergeant about taking the sick Marine's place. My first reaction was, "No way!" But as the night wore on and she looked at me with those big blue eyes, I finally gave in.

The next morning, I went to see the top sergeant and told him what I knew about the opening for sea school. I asked him to consider having me replace the Marine who had dropped out.

"How did you find out when I only heard about it this morning?" he asked.

I said, "Sir, my wife told me last night."

I told him what Alice had learned from her neighbor. "I really didn't want to ask you, sir, but last night those big blue eyes made me do it," I said.

He replied, "Well, this one takes the cake. But you're too small. You have to be at least 5 foot 8."

Well, that's exactly how tall I am. Once he determined I was tall enough, the sergeant placed me in the group headed to sea school. That meant I would be serving on a ship rather than on the ground and in the trenches. Hearing this made Alice very happy.

CAMP LEJEUNE, N. C.
Day, Night, Sunday and Holiday Pass

30 November, 194_4_

Pass Mrs. Alice Smith
Civilian wife Pvt. Wm. Smith
Into Camp Lejeune, N. C.

THIS PASS IS GOOD UNTIL 30 Jan 44

Provost Marshal

PASS NUMBER A-4712

7(308)45 N&Y JAX 8 29 44 10M   NAVMC-NRNC

William Smith (far left) and his high school buddies trained at Camp Lejeune in North Carolina before shipping out to war.

At left, the author appears in his Navy whites. The *Reedbird*, a WWII minesweeper (below), was reclassified in 1955.

Chilling Seas

A rogue winter hurricane tested the mettle of a Navy crew.

ROBERT REITH ◆ BETHEL PARK, PA

I was watching the Weather Channel when it mentioned a rare January event, a hurricane. My mind immediately went back to another January night, this one in 1955, when I was aboard a coastal minesweeper in the mid-Atlantic while a few miles away, Hurricane Alice was about to give us the ride of a lifetime.

I was on the USS *Reedbird*, MSC 51, under command of Lt. j.g. Robert R. Monroe. Monroe eventually would retire a vice admiral; the *Reedbird* was his first command. The four ships of our division left Charleston, South Carolina, in the morning en route to Panama City, Florida. The weather was overcast, and the seas were extremely high. As the seas grew higher, our division commander ordered a change in course so all ships were heading directly into the waves.

My first watch as officer of the deck was at 4 p.m. The waves were so steep that as we came down the crest of one wave, water would crash over our bow and the ship in front of us would disappear from view. As the ship in front crested the next wave, its two engine screws came completely out of the water.

By my next watch, at 4 a.m., the helmsman was having a difficult time keeping the ship on course. Suddenly, the *Reedbird* made a sharp swing to starboard (right), falling into the trough between the waves. Most of the crew, including the captain, were thrown from their bunks, and it really felt as if we would capsize. Then the engine room reported that the starboard propeller was jammed.

Captain Monroe rushed to the bridge as I got the ship back close to the correct heading. With one engine and our steering problems, we were losing sight of the other ships.

At some point during the night, we heard that the first ship had failed to secure a mooring

SHIP: U.S. NAVY MINESWEEPER, USS REEDBIRD (AMS-51)/US NAVAL INSTITUTE
WAR BONDS: WW/AP/SHUTTERSTOCK

> 66 *The waves were so steep that as we came down the crest of one wave, water would crash over our bow and the ship in front of us would disappear from view.* 99

line, which had likely washed overboard in the rough seas. That line must have become tangled in our propeller. If the same line caught in our other propeller, we would be at the mercy of the sea.

Mine Force headquarters in Charleston dispatched an ocean minesweeper—the largest ship in the Mine Force—to escort or tow us, but it would not reach the *Reedbird* until the following morning. In the meantime, headquarters notified Monroe's wife, who set up a prayer vigil among the officers' wives.

It was a long night. Finally, at dawn, we saw the ocean minesweeper—a beautiful sight.

Much later, I learned that Hurricane Alice had started in late December 1954 in the central Atlantic. Its track was well east of the *Reedbird*. We hadn't hit the rain zone, nor had we encountered hurricane-force winds.

But we had suffered, and thankfully survived, Alice's terrible waves.

WAR BONDS HELPED PAY for the U.S. military effort in WWII. Major marketing campaigns urged civilians to contribute their fair share. In 1942, undergrads from Barnard College in New York City held a friendly competition to advance the cause. Virginia Gildersleeve, dean of Barnard College, drops a dime into the faculty fishbowl, held by Pauline Washburn, head of the student committee, during a college-wide drive for war bonds.

In Command of His Surroundings

An older brother rises to the rank of hero in multiple ways.

DON WITTEN ◆ COLUMBIA, MD

My older brother, Bobby, spent time as a youth in the mid-1930s dressed in a black cape and hood made from an umbrella, helping those less fortunate than him. Wearing that costume, he could have been the inspiration for the original Batman character.

Years later, Robert became a real-life hero when he joined the Navy and qualified as a deep-sea diver. He rose in rank from seaman to ship's captain. He was commended for saving the life of a fellow seaman who was swept overboard from their submarine in rough seas. And he helped save several other seamen who were trapped in a fire aboard a submarine tied up next to his submarine service vessel, the USS *Florikan*, in 1962. Ten years later, he returned to the *Florikan* as the ship's captain before retiring in 1974.

During his 30-year naval career, Lt. Cmdr. Witten served as the ice navigation officer aboard the USS *Seadragon*, one of two nuclear submarines that made the first under-ice rendezvous at the North Pole in 1962.

Robert Lee Witten died in 2005. But my memories of him still prevail. I'll always remember my big brother as a true superhero.

Wearing his officer's uniform, Lt. Cmdr. Robert Witten strolls the deck of his ship, the USS *Florikan*. Right, stamps on a letter Witten sent in August 1962 herald the momentous North Pole rendezvous.

A Year in the Jungle

Friendships happened fast in those days. **DARRYLE PURCELL** ◆ BULLHEAD CITY, AZ

> *Dazed, bruised and embarrassed, I heard the formation fly off to find a better landing zone.*

Darryle spent most of 1966 in Vietnam.

It was 1966. The Huey formation flew in low over the Vietnam jungle.

"Any time now," the sergeant hollered.

The helicopters hovered a few feet over the top of what looked like thick shrubs. I stepped onto the strut, tossed the outer ring of a mortar into the air, grabbed the strut with one hand, swung down and dropped into the greenery.

About the same time, everyone realized those shrubs were the tops of some very thick, very tall jungle trees.

As I broke branches all the way to the ground, I remember thinking in third person, *Holy ****, Purcell!* Dazed, bruised and embarrassed, I heard the formation fly off to find a better landing zone. I gathered my rifle and equipment. The outer ring is probably still up in one of those trees.

Within a couple of hours the platoon found me. My friend Speer thought it was hilarious. He chuckled as he described my head vanishing into the foliage.

"Someday you'll look back on this and laugh," he said.

Speer used that line on me several times during my year

in Vietnam. And though I usually failed to agree with him at the time, he was eventually right.

I think of the night at the place we called Pleiku Pass when Sergeant Moore taught me that I wasn't a good poker player. It cost me every dollar I had, but the lesson was worth every cent. I haven't played poker since.

I think of the leader of our platoon, Lieutenant Hayes. Unlike most of the officers I had to deal with, Hayes was well-respected. He went on patrols with the rest of us. Other officers just sent out squads led by an E-5 (buck sergeant). Along with his M-16, Hayes carried a captured Thompson, which he planned to send back to the States so he could be "king of the block," as he liked to say.

I think of Carly, who was 17 when he came to 'Nam. When the rules changed, saying that a soldier had to be 18 to be sent into combat, Carly was offered the chance to return to the States. He decided to stay out his tour.

Carly was a good guitar player and tried to teach me the instrument when we were in base camp. I had paid 800 dong (about $8) for a Vietnamese guitar. At the time, I didn't know I had absolutely no musical ability. Anyone who listened in, however, did know.

Hayes, Moore and other officers and NCOs tolerated privates like Speer, Carly and me. We were kids. We did our jobs, made mistakes and always had a Bilko-like scheme going.

Speer and I finished our tours and returned stateside. Lieutenant Hayes, Sergeant Moore and Carly, like so many others, came home in bags.

Speer was right. Sometimes I think back and laugh about the good times. Sometimes I just think back.

David's friend Lee Roy Herron posthumously received the Navy Cross for extraordinary heroism.

Lee Roy Herron ❯

The Story Behind the Photograph

World travel and recognition can never replace the camaraderie of friends.

DAVID NELSON ◆ HOUSTON, TX

Years ago I received a copy of this iconic photograph taken during the Vietnam War. My buddy Lee Roy Herron is in the right foreground wearing glasses. The photo, which was taken on Jan. 26, 1969, by a Marine photographer at Fire Support Base Razor, appeared in the March 5, 1969, issue of *Navy Times* soon after Lee Roy's death on Feb. 22 of that year. Because I planned to start a scholarship fund in Lee Roy's name, I wanted to learn more about the photograph.

I tracked down the chaplain in the photo, Salvatore Rubino, a retired Navy captain, who told me: "The picture itself speaks thousands of words. There was utter desolation and destruction all around. There was the noise. Often during worship services, firepower was

called in and the guns would roar. We were tired, and some more exhausted than others. I recall that just before I served Communion, a helicopter approached to deliver ammunition. The wind generated by the rotor was so strong I had to cover the chalice with my hands to keep it from flying away. I was even afraid that the altar, made of five C-ration boxes and four ammo boxes, would bite the dust."

On June 20, 2010, I visited the National Museum of the Marine Corps in Quantico, Virginia. While touring the Vietnam War section, I noticed one wall devoted to honoring the Navy chaplains who had served in Vietnam. The top photo on the wall is this very one. What a fitting tribute to have the photo publicly displayed in such a spot.

Out to Sea

Soft voices across the water resonated with meaning.

FLOYD D. NORSKOG ◆ KANAB, UT

With the war raging in Korea, I joined the Marine Corps in May 1951. Two months later I was called to active duty and sent to the Marine Corps Recruit Depot (MCRD) in San Diego, California. A tenuous truce was called later that month, and the peace talks at Panmunjom began. Few of us believed the truce would last.

I was assigned to Platoon 209, billeted in quonset huts on the north side of the grounds. In the huts to our immediate west, another platoon was formed of members who were Chinese, Japanese, Filipino and Hawaiian, but no one of European descent.

They were a good group of soldiers. I suspect they'd had some training before arriving because they were skilled at marching and handling weapons, and from the beginning their discipline excelled. One thing stood out in this platoon: They sang as they marched. And they were really good. Imagine 52 men marching along singing in perfect harmony. They sang native Hawaiian songs and popular songs equally well.

That platoon went with us from boot camp to advance combat training at Camp Pendleton (near San Diego, California) to cold-weather training in the Sierras and finally back to Camp Pendleton for staging regiment, the final step before being sent overseas.

The peace talks were foundering, and the truce hung by a thread that could be broken by an accidental shot or the wrong set of words at the peace table.

On the eve of Dec. 7, we were trucked to the Naval Shipyard in San Diego and loaded aboard a MSTS (Military Sea Transportation Service) vessel, the USNS *Gordon*. Without a doubt, at 623 feet long, this was the biggest ship I had ever seen afloat.

Blackout conditions were in force, so no lights at all were allowed. Marines gathered on the deck, anywhere there was room. Voices were hushed as we awaited the inevitable. Finally, in the black of night, tugs pushed us away from the dock. Powerful rumbling told us the ship was coming to life. The *Gordon* was moving under its own power.

From the darkness of the ship we could see the lights of San Diego to the north, the naval shipyards nearby, and MCRD to the south. The lights formed a semicircle, and the *Gordon* moved toward the coal black horizon and the open sea. As we came closer to the mouth of the harbor, the soft voices of the singing platoon rose from the fantail of the ship.

The sound still rings in my ears: "Now is the hour that we must say goodbye. Soon we'll be sailing, far across the sea. While I'm away, oh then remember me."

> *Now is the hour that we must say goodbye. Soon we'll be sailing, far across the sea. While I'm away, oh then remember me.*

1955 Spring
Fuji Japan

Floyd's platoon went to Fuji, Japan, to join the Third Marine Division on its way to Korea.

Al's battalion arrived at Iwo Jima on Feb. 19, 1945, during the island's initial invasion. In a letter to his mother on Aug. 14, 1945, he informed her, "It looks like the war is just about over." Among the war mementos Al kept in a box (at right) were photos and his memoirs about landing on Iwo Jima while serving in the Army during World War II.

Long Wait for the Postman

A quickly written letter might be the only connection a family had to loved ones serving overseas. **ALBERT F. GALLO** ◆ GARDEN CITY SOUTH, NY

When my brothers, Joseph and Vincent, and I joined the war effort, my parents made us promise to write as often as possible. I was inducted into the Army on March 10, 1943, and for the first year and a half I wrote two or three times a week.

In late December 1944, after being stationed on Oahu, Hawaii, for nine months, we were sent to the Aiea staging area to await our next orders.

While there, we were allowed to write home, but we were instructed not to date our letters. During wartime, this helped keep our missions secure from the enemy.

Our ship left Hawaii on Jan. 21, 1945, stopping on Eniwetok and Kwajalein atolls and Guam on the way to our final destination. All the while, I wrote letters to my family and assumed they were dropped off on the islands and mailed back to the states.

We arrived at Iwo Jima on Feb. 19, prepared to land the next morning. Because there was so much wreckage on the beach, we were ordered to remain on ship. We could see and hear the fighting on the island, and while listening to the radio we learned our flag had been raised on Mount Suribachi. Sure enough, when we looked out, we could see the flag flying among the Marines gathered there.

During this time, we had been unable to write home. What we didn't know was that our letters had been held up since mid-December until after the invasion. I had assumed my family was getting everything I had written.

It took two months before we started receiving any mail. The first letters I got were from my sisters, who said the family hadn't heard from me in a while. Subsequent letters indicated they had received nothing from me in two weeks, three weeks, four weeks, then five weeks.

It took eight weeks before the mail finally caught up. I could only imagine what my parents were thinking back in Astoria, New York. We

> *My sisters told me my mother would wait anxiously every day in front of our house for the mailman to arrive.*

Iwo Jima veterans, clockwise from left, Charlie Wright, Leon Pluim, Adolph Borigama, Alex Kropovitch and Al Gallo

were a close family, and I knew how important it was for them to receive mail. With three sons in the war, our letters were their only lifeline to us.

My sisters told me my mother would wait anxiously every day in front of our house for the mailman to arrive. She would blame him for not having anything to deliver from me. I don't envy the postmen of that era. They did not have an easy time.

Naval photography kept Don working topside and out of the scary bowels of his ship, the USS *Independence*.

Simple Question, Big Decision

What happened during that 24-hour period may have saved one sailor's life.

DON MENDE ◆ RALEIGH, NC

When I was 16 back in Roanoke, Virginia, I got into some trouble. It was bad enough that I had to see a judge, who strongly suggested to my dad that I get some structure in my life. As an ex-Air Force pilot, Dad took that to heart and dragged me to the local Navy Reserve unit. Because I liked automobiles, I signed up as a machinist mate candidate and after two years of monthly meetings became a third-class machinist mate, having never worked on a ship.

After my graduation, I reported for active duty, and the Navy flew me to Japan to catch the USS *Independence* CVA 62 on its 1965 Vietnam tour. As I boarded the monster of a ship, I was convinced that drowning was in my immediate future.

A first-class machinist mate took me down several decks to a room filled with open bunks and dozens of dirty, oily new roomies. The sheets were filthy, and the noise and smells in that room were ghastly.

I told my guide that I was sure my momma didn't want her 19-year-old son down here, and that I needed to do something else, maybe with trucks. Then that wise old first-class machinist mate changed my life forever. He looked me straight in the eyes and said, "What do you think your momma would want you to be doing in this man's Navy?"

That made me think. My dad had done aerial photography while he was in the Air Force and was doing it now for a living. That seemed

The chief was tall and authoritative. I was scared beyond belief that if I screwed this up I was on my way back down to the bowels of the ship.

I got through the interview, and Chief Snyder handed me a roll of exposed film. He told me to process the film, make some 8x10 prints and show him that my photography skills were sufficient to warrant this coveted position.

So I stumbled through the dark room doors into a room lit with little red lights, where two men were working. I told them my story and said I had no idea what I was doing. The two guys, Randy Beck and Dale White, laughed and couldn't believe that I had convinced all these people, along with Chief Snyder, that I could be considered for the job.

Randy and Dale, who are still lifelong friends of mine, decided to help me with my little ruse and processed that roll of film, made some professional glossy prints and stood me in front of the dryer drum. When Chief Snyder came by, he would see me and the glossy prints and assume I had done the work.

That's exactly what happened! Chief Snyder came by and said that the processing and print quality were great and that if I was willing to lose my rank he would approve my transfer.

Of course I was low man on the totem pole and got all the worst duty—stuck with hot days on the flight deck, work in the AV room, late-night printing sessions, kitchen duty or whatever—but I was one happy buckaroo! The guys in the lab helped me along. I caught on pretty quickly. I eventually became a pretty good naval photographer.

Over the years I took classes in photography, chemicals, image composition, background, color and more. I have been fortunate to have made a living as a photographer for a good portion of my life. In the end, that 24-hour period aboard the *Independence* saved my life.

Heeding advice from a prudent shipmate, Don found a way to turn his fortunes around and launch a career in photography.

like a good job, so I told my new friend that if there were no trucks to work on, I was a good photographer. "Maybe I could do that," I said, knowing that I had never held a camera or taken a picture.

The old first-class laughed and then told me, "Photography is an impossible rating; there are so few openings and it's highly competitive." But he told me to see the personnel officer and tell him my story. "Maybe he can help you." After he left, I never saw him again.

The next day I went to see the P.O. I told him my story, and he called the chief in the photo lab to see if there was an opening.

Sure enough, there was, and Chief Snyder requested that I meet him in the lab to discuss.

BIG BROTHER CAME HOME

UPON RETURNING HOME after WWII, Ed Campbell bought his youngest brother, Calvin, his first bicycle. Calvin, of Charleston, Ilinois, shared this photo of the two saluting each other.

EUROPEAN EXPERIENCE

SPORTING WOODEN SHOES and pipes, Cpls. Eddy Johnson and Russell Collins relax for a moment during their adventures in Europe in 1952. Russell, of Umatilla, Florida, shared the photo.

HOME AGAIN

TAKEN IN LOS ANGELES, California, in 1944, this photo shows Tim Van Hemelryck's Uncle Jack and Aunt Donna home on leave.

66 *I'm standing here, third from left, with the brown shoes of attack squadron VA-115. Behind us is the airplane we flew, the TBM-3E Avenger torpedo bomber. Our brown shoes indicated we were Navy aviators.* 99

JOHN MAHON ◆ PORT RICHEY, FL

MOTORING MEMORIES

You never forget your first car or road trip, so cruise down memory lane with tales from behind the wheel. Start your engines!

CHAPTER 7

Hot Wheels

It was a whirlwind romance—with dual carbs. **JEAN ANDREW** • SAN DIEGO, CA

I met Ernest in 1953 at a Scottish gathering in San Diego, California. He asked if I would go out with him, but I lived 25 miles away in Encinitas, and he didn't have a car. The first time he came to my house, he took the city bus downtown, then the Greyhound bus to Encinitas. We just had time to walk to the theater to see a movie before he had to catch the bus for the long ride home.

After a few such trips, he decided he definitely needed wheels. One day, he showed up with a fire-engine red 1952 MG. I was surprised that my quiet, reserved boyfriend had chosen such a vehicle, but I didn't mind. It was a heady experience for a 16-year-old to be riding around in that little red sports car.

My mother, though, did have a problem with the car. We had come from Scotland six years earlier; she still viewed American men as too worldly. She had been happy with the boyfriend as long as he rode the bus, but not when he had a sports car.

Ernest was thrilled with his MG. He loved to put the top down and drive with his scarf streaming out the back, his jaunty cap clinging to his head. I was more inclined to slouch behind the windshield to keep my long hair from swirling into a tangled mess.

The car had its drawbacks. I don't remember it having a heater, and even a big coat didn't keep out the cold. When it rained we both had to yank the top into place, and Ernest helped the process along with a few choice words. And then there were the dual carburetors that were his pride and joy—and the bane of my existence. He spent hours tinkering with them. I still don't know what perfectly tuned carburetors sound like because Ernest never seemed to be able to get the MG's to that level.

We married in 1956, and I had to learn to drive the MG, which was nothing like my father's Ford. It had a stubby stick shift on the floor that my husband patiently explained had to be eased into gear. I ground my way through the gears on my first try.

When our first daughter came along in 1958, we traded in the MG for a sensible car. Ernest never lost his love for the MG; he remembered the feel of the wind on his face. I mostly remember the dreaded dual carbs.

Ernest zoomed his way into Jean's heart with this hot little roadster.

This Plymouth station wagon was a forerunner to the minivan.

The Original Family Vehicle

We've had this wooden-bodied 1941 Plymouth P12 Special Deluxe station wagon in the family since it was new, affectionately calling it the Banana Wagon. My uncle bought it at C.E. Fay Co. on Boston's famed Automobile Row along Commonwealth Avenue.

Its original invoice lists the car at $1,054, plus $26 for the optional "Comfort Master" heater. After a $450 trade-in for a 1937 Ford station wagon, my uncle paid $630.

The car still runs almost like new and has just over 56,000 original miles. It has a three-speed column shifter; the straight six-cylinder engine runs smoothly and has never been taken apart. In the cold weather the car rattles, but in humid summers, when the wood swells, it is tighter.

The Eddins blue car is largely unrestored and has always been garaged and maintained. The wood is original but was stripped of yellowed varnish and refinished in the early 1990s. The front seat was reupholstered, and several years ago we replaced the car's canvas roof.

This car once took children to school and towed small boats in the summer. But after it gently slid off the road one winter day in 1955, resulting in minor damage, my uncle retired it from daily service, wanting to preserve it. He continued to register it each year, and he drove it occasionally. I bought it from his widow in 1982.

With three rows of seats and capacity for eight passengers, the vehicle is the ancestor of the minivan, but it lacks modern frills. It's fun to drive, and it attracts lots of attention at car meets.

CHRISTOPHER MORSS ◆ SHERBORN, MA

MUSCLE MEMORY

I ONCE OWNED two of the best, most desirable muscle cars of all time, a '65 GTO convertible and a '68 GTO hardtop.

The '65's blue charcoal paint seemed to change colors with the sky. With its quick steering and stiff suspension, the performance was excellent. It was without doubt the fastest car I ever drove.

The '68 looked as if it was moving when it wasn't. The sound from the engine, even at idle, was as sweet as any I've heard.

Our son Todd rode with Mary Kay and me in the '68 "Goat" for three enjoyable years, but before our daughter Erin's birth in 1972, we traded it in for a '71 Catalina. Had it been financially feasible for us, I would have parked that '68 in the garage to enjoy to this very day. If only...

RON STURGA ◆ EDINBORO, PA

Pontiac GTO 1968

Pontiac GTO 1965

Third Wheel Came in Handy

The groom's Navy buddy helped cheer up a homesick bride.

IRVING DeMATTIES ◆ QUEENSBURY, NY

During my last months in the Navy in 1962, while stationed at Naval Facility Coos Head in Oregon, I was in a whirlwind courtship with my sweetheart, Linda Zumwalt. She was 18 and I was 24. But it was cut short by the Cuban missile crisis. A sonar specialist, I was ordered to report to Naval Facility Adak in Alaska to work with the system designed to detect Soviet submarines.

I'd just bought a 1954 Chevrolet, which I had to leave with Linda and her family. The missile crisis ended in late October, and I found out that I would be discharged.

Linda and I drove the Chevy to San Francisco, California, for my formal discharge on Jan. 2, 1963. That night, we married in San Jose, with my aunt and uncle as witnesses. Then it was back to North Bend, Oregon, to bid farewell to Linda's family.

A week later, we began a road trip to my hometown of Warrensburg, New York. It would turn out to be an unusual honeymoon—and not just because Linda cried all the way from Oregon to Nevada because she missed her family and friends. (I still marvel at the courage it took for her to go.)

Before we left, I'd run into a friend, John "O'B" O'Brien, who'd been discharged from the Navy the same day I was. O'B was from Boston and needed a way to get back home. Right away, I offered him a lift with us as far as Albany, New York, without consulting my new wife about the plan. (Amazingly, she still agreed to the trip.)

O'B was a nice-enough guy, but he was kind of a tightwad. He never wanted to spring for his own motel room. One night, it was bitter cold when we checked into a place on Route 66 near Amarillo, Texas. O'Brien refused to spend $10 for his own room, so he chilled in the Chevy. We drew the line at letting him stay in our room—after all, we were on our honeymoon.

But O'B could be useful on the road. He'd cheer up Linda by pretending he was playing

> **"** *Our journey included a dinner and show in Las Vegas and a half-day excursion to the Grand Canyon. We arrived in New York with $1.50 left in our trip fund.* **"**

the bagpipes. This involved pinching his nose while thumping his Adam's apple and emitting a high-pitched squeal.

Our journey included a dinner and show in Las Vegas and a half-day excursion to the Grand Canyon. We arrived in New York with $1.50 left in our trip fund.

Back home, I soon re-enlisted, and my Navy career lasted 23 years. Linda and I raised three beautiful daughters. Perhaps because of our first, long cross-country trip together, Linda and I got used to pulling up roots and starting over: We moved 14 times in 19 years.

In January 2009, 46 years after our big honeymoon trip, Linda and I bought a 1950 DeSoto because it looked a lot like our old Chevy. We think about our newlywed days whenever we drive it.

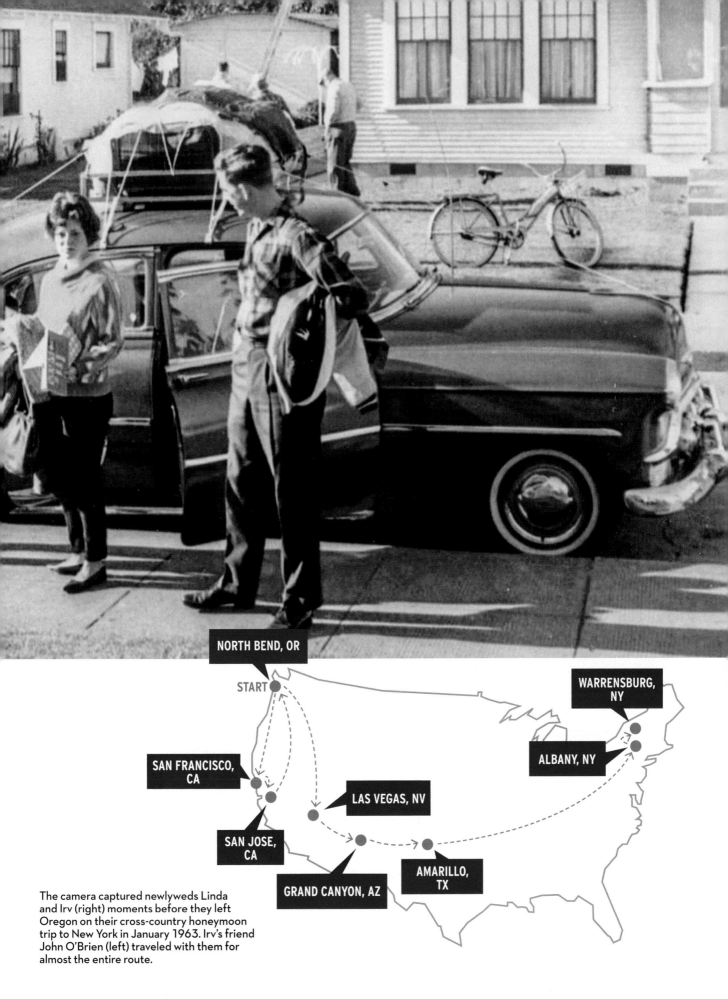

NORTH BEND, OR

START

WARRENSBURG, NY

SAN FRANCISCO, CA

ALBANY, NY

LAS VEGAS, NV

SAN JOSE, CA

GRAND CANYON, AZ

AMARILLO, TX

The camera captured newlyweds Linda and Irv (right) moments before they left Oregon on their cross-country honeymoon trip to New York in January 1963. Irv's friend John O'Brien (left) traveled with them for almost the entire route.

1969 Chevrolet Camaro

MY FATHER-IN-LAW owned a California dealership, Dana Chevrolet, in the 1960s that specialized in high-performance cars. In 2000, we found this Camaro, which came with its original bill showing it was a Dana car. We love it. That's my husband, David, and our daughter Elizabeth driving it home the day we bought it, and Elizabeth driving it herself in 2014.

PATRICIA DOSKI
PALOS VERDES PENINSULA, CA

No Car, No Keys, No Problem

In the early '70s, I owned a beat-up blue 1961 Buick Electra that had a peculiar quirk: It could be started and driven without the key if you simply turned the ignition switch on the steering column.

I was dating a West Point cadet then. One day my date and I were at the on-post movie theater. Another cadet, who because he was dating my best friend knew the car's little secret, spied my Buick in the parking lot and decided to borrow it to chauffeur his date.

When I returned to the parking lot after the movie, an apprehensive plebe cadet was standing at ease—rather, I should say, ill at ease—in the space where I had parked my car.

But the car was not there. The plebe, who was clearly uncomfortable, nevertheless carried out the order that the borrower had given him: He snapped to attention, sharply saluted and barked, "Ma'am! Cadet Walter has commandeered your car, and it will be returned at 1630 (4:30) with a full tank of gas!"

And it was.

GIOIA GRASSO ◆ WEST LEBANON, NH

> *While my date and I were at the movie theater, another cadet spied my Buick in the lot and decided to borrow it.*

Buicks from the early '60s were sleek, but the author's also had a tricky ignition.

Pretty in Power

The need for speed knows no age limit. **LINDA DILLS** ◆ TUCSON, AZ

My mother, Lorraine Fischer, bought this gorgeous 1978 Chevrolet Monte Carlo when she was in her 60s. It actually was her second choice. She first picked out a Chevy Nova but returned it, saying "it had trouble making it up a hill." She wanted something with more power. This two-tone beauty caught her eye, and it was love at first sight. It turned out to have all the power she wanted.

The car never left our hometown, but she did rack up over 98,000 miles going to the local fabric store, post office, church and her favorite drive-in restaurant, Taco Bell. She had fun coming to a traffic stop next to some young fellows. They'd yell out their car window, "Hey lady, want to sell that car?"

"No way!" was always her answer. Then she'd hit the gas and leave them in her dust.

Mom was something of a daredevil. At 21 she learned to fly, and she earned her pilot's license in 1940. During World War II she worked for the military bureau of the Milwaukee Road rail line, directing soldiers to their points of departure. She also worked as a stenotypist (I still have her stenotype machine). Later on, she enjoyed working as a teacher's aide; she loved helping the children.

She drove the car for 30 years, until she was well into her 90s. Just before she passed away at 97, she could no longer drive. I took the wheel for her, but I knew she would rather be the pilot. She fed her need for speed by becoming a regular viewer of NASCAR races on TV.

My mother is gone now and I miss her, but I'm happy to report that her car found another owner who loves it as much as Mom did.

Lorraine shows off her 1978 Chevrolet Monte Carlo.

Pat Greene enjoyed his 1939 Dodge Business Coupe.

Loved from Afar, 'Miss Cettie' Was a Special Gift

His wife surprised him with a dream car. **PAT GREENE** ◆ MOUNTAIN CITY, TN

As I arrived home from a game of golf in October 1998, my wife, Mary, came out to meet me. "I did something today I have never done before in my life," she said. She grinned. "I bought a car."

It wasn't just any car. It was a vehicle I had admired for a long time.

For many years I owned a barbershop in our small Tennessee town, and I'd often see an old car parked on the street near the shop. One day I noticed an older woman getting out of it and I asked her if she would mind if I had a closer look at her Dodge Business Coupe. "You can look all you want," she said, "but I'll tell you right now, it's not for sale."

The woman was Cettie Keys, a retired teacher who was very particular about her car, which she had bought new in Marion, Virginia, for $825. I loved that vehicle.

A few decades later, my wife was walking with our new neighbors, Ted and Carol, a couple with

whom Mary had graduated from high school many years before. During the walk, the subject of old cars came up, and Mary related the story of Cettie Keys' car.

Incredibly, through a quite complex set of circumstances, Ted had become the owner of the car after Miss Keys died. At that very moment, it was parked in Ted's garage.

After just a little negotiating with Ted, Mary bought the car. What an amazing surprise! I was so proud to drive it home.

We nicknamed the car "Miss Cettie." It came with most of its original papers, including the purchase invoice and a booklet with oil-change records, as well as Cettie Keys' license plates, umbrella and a set of reading glasses—all treasures we kept in the big trunk.

On Christmas Eve 2012, our daughter Kim became the fourth owner of Miss Cettie. We wanted to be sure that it and Miss Keys' legacy would be well cared for.

He Soared with Confidence on a Cushman Eagle

We lived in Little Rock, Arkansas, when I was a boy. When I turned 12, my father bought me a 1952 Barrel Spring Cushman Eagle for my birthday. With its customized chrome gas tank and fenders, it was the most beautiful thing I had ever seen.

That motor scooter gave me the kind of freedom few 12-year-olds had. I just about drove the wheels off it. I went anywhere and everywhere, whenever I wanted. I have many, many memories about that scooter, but a few stand out.

I used it for my paper route, so I needed gas. My papers were dropped off each morning at a Gulf station with eight pumps. In those days, they didn't lock up the pumps, they just turned them off each night. I got the bright idea to drain the pump hoses into my scooter. By doing that every morning, I very seldom had to buy gas, even though it was only 25 cents a gallon.

I also rode around with my best friend, Fred. My scooter didn't have a passenger seat, just a hard metal bar rack, which is where Fred sat. Believe me, we went on adventures. And with Fred on the back I would look for every chughole

Jim covered the county on his trusty motor scooter.

and bump I could find. To this day, Fred complains about what those rides did to his rump.

A few years later, I wanted to see what made my scooter tick, so I took it completely apart. After I got it back together, I had a coffee can full of leftover parts. But it still ran!

As I look back on it, I realize that scooter had a major influence on my life. It gave me a love of tools and anything mechanical. And it gave me a measure of confidence and independence that I have to this day.

JIM BEATH ◆ BOERNE, TX

VINTAGE ADS

BY THE '60s, GULFPRIDE offered two classes of oil, Gulfpride Single-G and Gulfpride Motor. Drivers could now choose to customize the weight of their oil or buy one that was "just right" for all terrains and climates.

....

MOBIL SPEAKS TO THE mechanically inclined consumer by touting a smoother ride, lower upkeep costs and a longer-lasting engine. What more could a driver ask for?

1963

Three Decades Later, a Treasured Car Comes Home

He thought he'd never see that Camaro again. He was wrong.

DENNIS LAYMAN ◆ PEMBERVILLE, OH

After buying back his old Camaro, Dennis restored it to get it as close as possible to the car he bought in '69.

After I graduated from junior college in 1968, I was back home in Pemberville and decided it was time to buy the Camaro I'd always wanted. I mulled over the possible choices for the '69 models, and picked the best one of all—the Super Sport (SS) package for the power and the Rally Sport (RS) trim for the luxury features like covered headlights, custom interior and rosewood steering wheel.

I was 19. I had enough for a down payment but needed my dad's help to get a bank loan. I wanted the 396-cubic-inch, 350-horsepower engine, but my father refused to co-sign my loan if I got that option. So I settled for 350 cubic inches and 300 hp.

I paid about $3,600 for the Camaro, which was delivered on March 18, 1969. I was so excited that I could barely work the four-speed shift to get it home, which was less than a mile from the dealer.

I drove my Camaro every day and drag-raced the country roads at night, mostly with friends who also had muscle cars. But in 1974, with my wife pregnant, we decided that we needed a family car. I sold my beloved Camaro to a young man who lived a few miles away. He had it for a while until he sold it to someone else. I lost track of the car after that, assuming it was long gone or rusting away in a junkyard somewhere.

But in the summer of 1998, a car caught my eye at a small local show. It was a 1969 SS/RS Camaro with a black vinyl top and a metallic blue body. It had the same black custom interior, rosewood steering wheel, console and gauges as my old '69 SS/RS. It even had a Hurst T-handle on the gear shift lever, which I had installed on my car years ago. The woman who owned it lived about 15 miles from me. Just about the only difference between her car and my old one, I told her, was the color.

When she replied that her car used to be silver-gray, my heart started to pound hard. I told her who I'd sold mine to and she smiled. His name was on an old vehicle registration for the Camaro that she kept in the glove box.

The Camaro had lived an interesting life with her: She'd replaced the engine and raced the car at area drag strips, winning several trophies.

I called her every spring for years asking if she'd sell it to me, but she always refused. Finally, in 2007, she was ready. The day I drove the Camaro home, I was as excited as I'd been on March 18, 1969.

These days, I drive the car about 600 miles a year, mostly to shows in the summer. I never drive it in the winter, and I store it in a heated building. I won't let it get away from me again.

Charging Ahead

The car was so bad, it was good.

DAN McCALLUM ◆ HENRIETTA, TX

Along with every other young car buff in Haltom City, Texas, in 1968, I just had to see *Bullitt* starring Steve McQueen. I was 15 at the time. All that my friends could talk about was the green Mustang fastback that McQueen drove.

But I fell in love with the 1968 black-on-black Dodge Charger the bad guys drove. At the sound of that engine, I decided that if I ever got the chance, I was going to get a car like that.

My yearning for a Charger grew worse when, a short time after I saw the movie, a friend of the family came to my father's house at Christmas driving a 1968 Charger R/T. He saw me really checking out his car and took me for a ride, showing me what it could do. Yep, I was hooked all right.

Fast forward to the mid-1970s and I finally got my chance. I found a black-on-black 1968 Charger R/T, just like the one in the movie. Sure it was fast, but I was a mechanic at the time, so I

The bad guys' Charger in *Bullitt* captured Dan's fancy so much that he eventually found one of his own.

modified it to make it faster. It was also beautiful.

That was the car I enjoyed the most in my lifetime. Like most former hot-rodders who sold their old muscle, I wish I still had it. That Charger made for a lot of good memories.

GO, SPEED RACER, GO!

ROUNDING TURN 3 in the black-and-white photo, Ralph Bush of Arroyo Grande, California, sits in his Singer SM1500 in the Sports Car Club of America race in June 1965 at the Pomona fairgrounds track in Pomona, California. "I've been road-racing sports cars for more than 60 years," Ralph writes. He was still racing into his 80s—the full-color photo shows him rounding a turn, this time in a Thunder Roadster during the National Auto Sport Association race at Road Atlanta, Braselton, Georgia, in December 2015.

> *I've been road-racing sports cars for more than 60 years.*

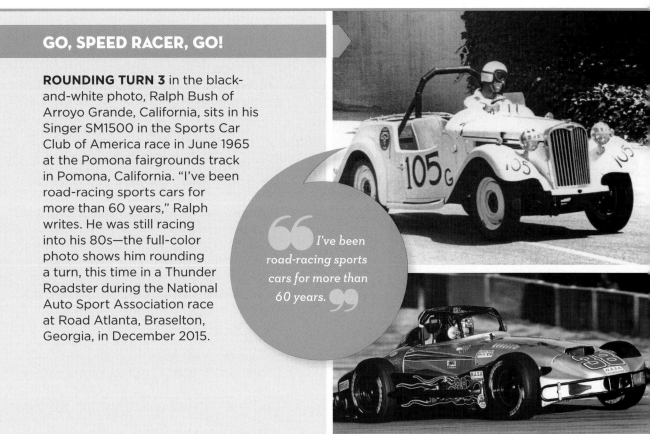

WHAT'S THAT EDSEL PROMO
worth today? Edsel dealers used turquoise-and-white promos in the test-drive giveaway. Aluminum Model Toys Inc. (AMT), a toy manufacturer, made Edsel promos in a variety of factory colors for dealer use but switched up color combinations or treatments on cars sold in toy stores.

1935 GMC Patrol Wagon

It's Edsel Showtime on the Road

ROAD-CHECK THE BIG ONE GET A LITTLE ONE FREE

$2 precision scale model Edsel yours as a gift when you take the test drive of a lifetime!

(Offer limited to adults only)

In the medium-priced field
THE ONE THAT'S REALLY NEW IS THE LOWEST PRICED, TOO!

Ask for

for a real deal — as little as

From Prisoners to Parades

Milwaukee Police Post 415 of the American Legion is an organization of armed forces veterans who have also served in our city's police department. In 1941, the post acquired an original Milwaukee police vehicle, a 1935 GMC Patrol Wagon, to make appearances in parades, car shows and other various civic functions.

A troupe of Keystone Kops—active and retired officers who wear authentic police uniforms dating to the 1880s—often accompanies the wagon on parades, much to the delight of the crowds.

In its original police role, the wagon transported prisoners. Since becoming Legion property, its passengers have included singer Eddie Fisher and the actors Ernest Borgnine and Mark Harmon. When Harmon starred in the 1991 TV movie *Dillinger*, our wagon had a supporting role.

Over the years Post 415 has put the vehicle to such good use that it has broken down many times. We replaced the six-cylinder engine about six years ago with a period-correct motor that was two years older than the one that died. The radiator blew in 2015 and had to be rebuilt. The post replaced the side windows with screens for parade use, and the once-black truck was repainted dark blue.

Everything else is original except for the directional lights, the hand-printed lettering and the American Legion emblems on the doors.

DONALD BROCKMAN ◆ MILWAUKEE, WI

They'll know you've *arrived*
when you drive up in an Edsel

It shows them all what *new* really means —outside, inside, and on the road!

1958
EDSEL

A SPRING AD CAMPAIGN
announced "The Edsel is Coming" five months before the car's release. Once unveiled, the vehicle got a lot of lookers—but buyers, not so much.

Driving with Daddy

A nod of approval was all she needed. **ANN McDONALD** • SHAWNEE, OK

These days, North Kickapoo Street in Shawnee, Oklahoma, is a four-lane road leading out to the interstate, and lined with all kinds of places to eat and shop. But in the mid-1950s, it was just a gravel country road, the perfect place for our daddies to teach us how to drive.

We didn't have driver's education at Shawnee High School; we were on our own. Mom took me to pick up an instruction manual. I was the oldest of my friends, so we were excited at the prospect of a whole new world opening up. We'd have freedom to get around. Best of all, we could go to the Starlite Drive-In theater on 50-cents-a-carload night. We'd have it made.

Mom let me back our 1949 Ford out of the garage a few times to get used to the clutch and gearshift. I got familiar with the motion but was hardly ready for my road test.

Finally, the day came for Daddy to give me a real lesson. He drove out to the end of the paved section of Kickapoo Street and across to where

> " *I was feeling pretty good as I came to a stop and looked to Daddy for approval.* "

the gravel started. My daddy had come from a family of 10, and they had been farmers in Oklahoma during the Dust Bowl. There was only one way to do things, and that was the right way.

Compliments were rare, so when he muttered his approval it was special. I really didn't want to experience his glare if I ground the clutch or if the car jerked as I tried to get it going.

I took a deep breath, slowly let out the clutch, pushed the stick into second gear, eased down the road, and then carefully moved into third gear. He had me stop and repeat the procedure two or three more times until I came to the end of the section. I was feeling pretty good as I came to a stop and looked to Daddy for approval.

He glared at me and then barked, "You've been driving, haven't you?"

He must have thought I'd been practicing in somebody else's car. I quickly explained that my training was all on the up-and-up.

That was 60 years ago. I can still see the nod he gave me when he said, "Well, you did good."

The trusty '49 Ford that Ann took over when she got her license

In 1960, Sherman bought this blue and white beauty and his friend bought a red Corvette on the same day and from the same salesman.

> " The salesman probably never again sold two Corvettes on the same day. "

Little Twin Corvettes

Double deal for two customers made it a day to remember.

SHERMAN SMALLWOOD ◆ VINTON, VA

My first experience with a Corvette was in 1959. My father-in-law had a business acquaintance, a lawyer named Arnold, who owned a red 1958 model. Arnold's college-age son was coming home for Memorial Day weekend, and Arnold didn't want him driving the Corvette, so he left the car with my father-in-law for safekeeping. I got to drive the Vette and was quite impressed. I decided I absolutely had to have one.

In 1960, my wife, Jeanette, and I were working for a general contractor at the Greenbriar Hotel in White Sulphur Springs, West Virginia. She was in the payroll office and I was in the field. We spent a weekend in Roanoke, Virginia, and while she visited the hairdresser, I went to the Chevy dealer. He had two Corvettes on display, a red one with a white top and cove and a solid black one. When I picked up Jeanette and told her where I had been, she insisted we return and look some more.

At work on Monday, Jeanette told another clerk, Henry, about the cars. He wanted to rush back to Roanoke right away to look at them. We did, but Henry and his wife were riding with us, and the salesman wouldn't discuss a trade with Henry until he could bring in his own car. So we all returned to the dealership the following Saturday; this time Henry drove himself.

We made that salesman's day! Henry bought the red Vette and I ordered a light blue one with a white top and cove. The salesman probably never again sold two Corvettes on the same day.

We had a lot of fun and enjoyed getting together with several other couples, parading around, stopping as a group at a restaurant or just showing off. We got a lot of attention—some friendly waves and some envious looks.

But the Corvette could be inconvenient if you didn't have a second, larger vehicle. We toughed it out for about a year and a half before we went back to a more sensible car, a 1962 Impala SS.

Caught in a Jamb

Tight spaces were not her friend.

LORRAINE HAWKINSON ◆ OREGON, WI

"You're sure in there," the garage man said, standing near his tow truck. I knew that already. If I weren't "in there," I would not have called him.

We both considered my predicament. I'd parked too close to the wall, so the passenger side of my car was lodged behind the frame of the garage door. I couldn't back out and I couldn't pull up.

How had this happened? After all, we have a large double garage. There should have been plenty of room. But I have to admit that it wasn't the first time I'd done this. In the past, by maneuvering the car a few inches forward and back, I'd been able to ease it far enough to clear the doorjamb.

The situation this time was out of hand. I'd tried my old trick of inching the car 2 inches forward then 2 inches back, but it struck the wall at both points and remained resolutely behind the jamb. I'd tried jacking up the car—at the same time learning how to use the new scissors jack—but that made it tip closer to the wall with a scratchy sound that hurt my ears. I'd even thought of trying to bounce the car sideways by pumping vigorously on the rear bumper. No luck.

I was supposed to be at my desk at a reasonable hour and, unlike my car, time was not standing still. I'd considered staying home (I was feeling quite sick), but the thought of my husband seeing the car in such an impossible position canceled that idea quickly.

Finally, admitting defeat, I called Schmity's. After a series of squats and deep bends, along with some mysterious clucking, the tow truck driver decided that a low winch on the rear axle at a 90-degree angle would be the thing to try.

"Get in and set the brakes real tight and hold them," the fellow ordered.

Slowly the heavy cable tightened and the car began to inch to the left. It worked!

"Whoopee!" I hollered.

I thanked the man. I thanked him again. And I paid him. I paid him an enormous amount.

All day long I thought, *I'll never tell my husband about this as long as I live.* But by the time I got home, the whole thing seemed kind of funny. So I told him.

And would you believe it? The grumpy sorehead didn't think it was one bit funny.

AS SOON AS I TURNED 16 in 1963, I got my driver's license. My dad had taught me on our family's 1958 Chrysler, with its push-button transmission. It was chartreuse green with enormous fin fenders.

One of the first times I took this huge automobile out by myself was to help my 10-year-old sister, Arnis, deliver May baskets. We drove around the block to her friend's house, our first stop. As I backed out of that driveway, one of the fancy fins hung up on a fire hydrant. It took three men and two car jacks to get it off.

We drove straight home after that, and Arnis delivered the rest of her baskets on foot. Here, Arnis and I stand with our mom, Jeanne Hunt, in front of the Chrysler in 1961.

GAYLE HUNT MATZ
BROOKINGS, SD

AN OLD LOVE FOUND

BETWEEN THE AGES of 16 and 18, Sam Weirbach of Redmond, Washington, got 17 speeding tickets. Over the years he used his ticket experience to help young men understand that choices have consequences. "One of those young men was my son Nate," says Sam. "When he was a teenager, Nate secretly planned with his mother to find me a '68 Camaro, the car I dreamed of as a young man. When they finally found one, my wife told me to check it out because 'your son thinks you have suffered enough.'"

Today, 20 years later, it is still a dream of Sam's to drive. Is it fast? Yes. But he has not received one speeding ticket driving it.

Chevrolet Camaro 1968

Old Warhorse Still in Fighting Trim

Lavell's 1955 Willys M38A1 jeep

Do you remember playing army as a kid? Invading your buddy's territory with plastic soldiers and little olive green trucks? My dream to own a military vehicle dates to those carefree days growing up in Lowesville, North Carolina.

My dad, Pap, bought this 1955 Willys M38A1 jeep at an estate auction several years ago. An Air Force veteran and the commander of the American Legion post in Boone, North Carolina, Pap wanted it mainly for parades.

I was sure he'd never part with it, but then Pap offered to sell it to me so he could buy a 1930 Model A Ford. The small green plastic toy of my youth had now been upgraded to the real McCoy.

This heavy-duty piece of American military history is powered by a four-cylinder Hurricane F-head 134-cubic-inch engine, pushing 72 horsepower. It's mated to a T-90 three-speed transmission, and it has a 24-volt electrical system and four-wheel drive.

The model also came with an underwater ventilating system. It can drive through water over 6 feet deep.

Because of its military heritage, the jeep had no vehicle identification number. After an involved process with the Division of Motor Vehicles, the utility truck, manufactured over six decades ago, got its first VIN and title in November 2014.

Gomer, as we affectionately call it, always gets a lot of attention, especially from veterans. Sporting its original olive drab, Gomer rolls on military NDT (nondirectional tread) 7-by-16-inch tires on military standard drop-center 16-inch wheels.

I'm thrilled to be the caretaker of such a rare piece of Americana. That it was Pap's makes it all the more special.

LAVELL HALL ◆ LINCOLNTON, NC

Her Name Is Lola, and She's a Showgirl

Bronze Mach 1 was part of a package deal, and she's still around today. **JAN HARTZOG** ◆ MISSION, TX

When I was 15, my next-door neighbor Gary got a 1971 Mustang Mach 1 as a graduation present. It was love at first sight for me. Growing up in the muscle car era, I had lots of favorites, from Chargers to Camaros, but the Mach 1 was in a whole different category. When I saw that sleek silver beauty with black racing stripes, I decided that someday I would own one.

In May 1976 I happened to pass a car lot and saw a bronze 1973 Mach 1. I couldn't turn around and get back to that lot fast enough. I talked my dad into co-signing the $3,000 loan, and a couple of days later that baby was mine. I named her Lola after the showgirl in Barry Manilow's "Copacabana (At the Copa)."

My boyfriend proposed to me in 1977, and I told him it was a package deal—me, my car and my springer spaniel, Brandy. He was fine with it. I'm fortunate that he was because he's a mechanical genius who keeps Lola in top shape.

When my kids were in junior high they were mortified if I used my "old car," as they called her,

> ❝ *I talked my dad into co-signing the $3,000 loan, and a couple of days later that baby was mine.* ❞

to take them to school. They'd beg to get out before we reached the school so they wouldn't be seen with her.

But once my son got to high school, my car suddenly became "pretty cool," and he was always asking to drive her. I'd just tell him, "Oh, you don't want to drive that old car." I never did let him drive her to school, but I did let him drive her to his wedding.

In 2005, we had Lola repainted in her original color (saddle bronze) and she's as beautiful now as the day I got her 41 years ago.

These days she doesn't get driven too much—mainly to cruise-ins, to car shows and on the occasional joy ride—but I still love the feeling I get every time I drive her.

My daughter summed it up best a few years ago when she said, "Wow, Mom, your generation had the cool music and cool cars!"

Jan loves to take Lola out for a cruise.

Dale is proud of his 1968 AMC Rebel SST, similar to the one his dad had.

Sporty Hardtop Comes Full Circle

After tagging along on shopping trip for the family car when he was young, he finds a similar car years later. **DALE VEVERKA** ◆ INDEPENDENCE, OH

Searching for a good deal on a 1968 demonstrator model, my father took me with him to a local car lot during the summer of 1969. As I wandered off to gaze longingly at a cool two-seater on the showroom floor, Dad bought a sensible four-door AMC Rebel sedan.

A few years later, I was finally entrusted with the keys to Dad's car. Away to college I went, taking the now middle-aged Rebel on a field trip to rural Ontario. On that trip, my classmates and I learned that the car could reach excessive speeds, even with four of us and all of our luggage aboard.

Fast-forward a number of years. I finally bought the two-seater I had coveted years earlier. My oldest daughter had purchased a similar car and was storing it in a neighbor's garage. A crew of roofers was working on the house next door, and her car caught the foreman's eye. He mentioned to her that he had a vintage car by the same maker to sell.

When my daughter told me about it, I was hoping the car would be a dog, too far away to view or already sold, as my garage was overflowing with half a dozen cars. But I rang up the roofer and made an appointment to see it.

It turned out to be the same model my dad had bought at the dealer in 1969, though this was the two-door version. It boasted top-of-the-line trim, a spotless interior, a V-8 engine and only 35,000 miles on the odometer. Of course I bought it.

With new paint and some minor restoration work, the sporty hardtop isn't exactly what Dad had in mind when he took me shopping for a family car back in 1969. But it still brings me full circle to that day so long ago.

From a Golden Era of Design

Enormous tail fins meet sleek atomic touches. **GARY PIETRANIEC** ◆ BRIGHTON, MI

As a kid growing up near the corner of Rosemont and Warren in Detroit, I used to hang around the older guys and their hot rods. Those guys were generous to a squirt like me—they'd let me sit in their cars and pretend I was driving and shifting gears. They had '49 Fords, '50s Chevrolets and old pickup trucks. I know that was the beginning of my love of hot-rodding.

I've had several classic cars since those childhood days, but this one is my favorite. I pursued this red beauty for almost three years before the man who'd owned it for 19 years decided to sell it when he moved into a condo. This '59 Chevy Impala Sport Coupe is a beautiful, sleek automobile, with styling all its own. It comes from an era when there was a passion for design, a special point in time when the outrageous tail fins of the 1950s met the Space Age, with its rocket and Sputnik design cues.

I take it to most of the local car spots and cruises, and I've entered it in a few shows, including the Motor Muster at the historic Greenfield Village in Dearborn, Michigan.

But the best times are hanging out with other die-hard hot-rodders at local '50s and '60s diners and drive-ins. The minute you pull into the parking lot, with the AM radio blaring Jackie Wilson's "Lonely Teardrops" on the oldies station and the smell of burgers and sauteed onions on the grill, you're back in the good old days. And I'm back at Rosemont and Warren, sitting in a '49 Ford, pretending to drive, without a worry in the world.

Gary's atomic beauty is a 1959 Chevy Impala Sport Coupe.

RIDING THE OPEN ROAD

BACK FROM WWII where he served as a C-47 crew chief, John Flannagan steadies his Harley-Davidson in about 1947 and gets ready to cruise with his bride-to-be, Bernice Marhefka. John Flannagan Jr. of Clinton, Massachusetts, shared the photo.

IT HAPPENED ONE AFTERNOON

DOING AN IMITATION of Clark Gable and Claudette Colbert in *It Happened One Night,* friends Bob Ambrose and Elayne Dion pose together. Elayne, who lives in Wilbur-by-the-Sea, Florida, says her brother Paul's 1951 Studebaker Champion convertible in back was getting a flat tire replaced.

RACING DUO

ART AND JAN PETERSON of Rialto, California, pose with their 1969 GTO, which they've been running on the track since 1970. "Our kids grew up at the races," Art says.

A TIGER ON THEIR TANK

HERE ARE JODI AND SCOTT in 1970 standing next to a Volkswagen Beetle their father had painted with different animal prints. Doris LaMarr of Magnolia, Texas, shared the photo.

CATCHING A RIDE

IN 1941, when the summer heat was intolerable, Norma M. Butts' dad drove the family to Montauk Point on Long Island Sound, Suffolk County, New York. Norma's sister Nina, is on the running board, and Norma, now of Tarzana, California, peeks out from the backseat.

DAIRY DELIVERY

ERNIE BERTRAM, 10, poses with the Decker's Dairy truck in front of the Bertram store in Hightstown, New Jersey, in 1933. Ernie's son Bruce, of South River, New Jersey, says the bottle-shaped vehicle was popular in parades and at events.

Her Chevy's Secret Life as a Hot Rod

Mother was not happy when her car's oil began to disappear quickly. Then she discovered the culprit. **MARY CHATMAN** ◆ PUXICO, MO

Mom didn't know her son was a lord of the blacktop in her beloved new car.

My mother, Bess Straughan, had just bought a new Chevy in 1955—and was so proud of it. My brother Joe, who was 16 at the time, was itching to drive it. Mom was hesitant, but after a lengthy lecture about speed, and making him promise not to leave the city limits or drive over 40 mph, she let him take her car for the evening.

Soon Joe was driving the Chevy quite regularly.

One day, Mom noticed the car was going through oil. She couldn't figure out what was causing the trouble, so she made an appointment for the dealer to check it out. Something was wrong, she was sure—the dealer was really going to hear from her.

The appointment was for a Monday. On the Saturday before, she drove to the grocery store. She was walking out with her purchases, helped by one of the store's teenage clerks, who asked her which car was hers. Mom pointed to her aqua and cream Chevy.

"Wow," the clerk said. "Is that yours? That's the fastest car in town!"

Apparently Joe had been taking Mom's Chevy out to a long stretch of Highway 32 where teenagers regularly drag raced—and he was winning most of the time.

That night, Mom canceled her appointment with the dealer. And Joe's short-lived reign as a drag king ended abruptly.

HANG ON TIGHT

A 1937 DODGE PULLS schoolboys on a blood-curdling ride in the snow in Goodells, Michigan, in about 1958. "My father, Sandy, kept the car as a service vehicle at his gas station," says Jim Sanderson, now of nearby Port Huron. "In the winter, we drove the car around the field playing this game. The object was to dump anyone riding. Dad provided us all the ropes, chains and tires."

During WWII, I got my driver's license on my 14th birthday. I attended Lodi High School in Lodi, California, and used our 1917 red Saxon for transportation. The Saxon, a six-cylinder competitor to the Ford Model T, had no door, top or fenders. But my rolled-up Levi's were a classic. ❞

TOM BRITZMAN • EAST GARRISON, CA

FOR THE LOVE OF THE GAME

*Three cheers
for the home team!
No matter the sport,
there's a camaraderie
and spirit around these
favorite pastimes.*

CHAPTER 8

I Played for the Cornhuskers

Although I have never been what you'd call athletic, I like to tell friends that I played in the Cotton Bowl, the Orange Bowl and the Sugar Bowl. I did—I played saxophone. My time at the University of Nebraska (1964-'68) was the period when Coach Bob Devaney brought the Cornhusker football team to national prominence.

Unfortunately, the Huskers lost all three games, first to the Arkansas Razorbacks and then twice to Alabama's Crimson Tide. To this day, I still find myself cringing when I hear "Woo pig sooie!" or "Roll Tide!"

STEVE GOLD ◆ CORONA, CA

The Nebraska marching band (below) looks sharp in 1967. Steve can't tell which of the sax players he is, but "I'm one of them," he says. At left, the band revs up the crowd at a pep rally before the 1965 Cotton Bowl.

Everything's Coming Up Rose Bowl

The 1958 Rose Bowl game pitted the Ducks of the University of Oregon against the Ohio State University Buckeyes. California sportswriters were calling it the "worst mismatch of the ages," and oddsmakers had the "Ugly Ducklings" a 19-point underdog.

But the sportswriters were wrong. Final score: Ohio State 10, Oregon 7. Oregon fans were so jubilant that you'd have thought the Ducks had won.

I was secretary to the Oregon football coaching staff and was so proud of my bosses and the team members. They were winners in my playbook!

REBECCA TOWLER FALKNER ◆ EL PASO, TX

BOWL GAME FACTS

SWEET FACT: The last Tulane Stadium Sugar Bowl was in 1974. Today the game is played at the Mercedes-Benz Superdome.

COTTON FACT: The Cotton Bowl Classic marked its 82nd game on Dec. 29, 2017.

TART FACT: The Citrus Bowl first started in 1947 as the Tangerine Bowl.

The Oregon Ducks, foreground, warm up before the Rose Bowl game against Ohio State on New Year's Day 1958.

THANKS TO HIS DAD, my boyfriend had free tickets to the Alabama-Arkansas Sugar Bowl game in 1962.

A rare New Orleans snowfall from the day before had melted, but it was still very cold. The game was in Tulane Stadium, an open-air facility. In a wool dress, heels and nylon stockings, I hadn't dressed for the weather. I was amazed to see icicles on the benches.

Alabama won 10-3 to finish undefeated under Coach Bear Bryant. I walked on shaky legs back to Joe's car. I took out a mirror to primp—and immediately wished that my nose was not so red.

Joe didn't mind; he became my husband.

CAROLYN PONS ◆ LAFAYETTE, LA

....

I GOT MY LOVE OF FOOTBALL from my late husband. When the Penn State Nittany Lions got into the Citrus Bowl in 1988, I asked a friend who'd lost her husband, too, to go to the game with me in Orlando, Florida.

My dear Lions lost 35-10 to the Clemson Tigers, so we looked to Disney World for better things. That turned out to be the highlight of the trip, though not in the way you'd expect: We got stranded in the giant golf ball (Spaceship Earth) at Epcot when the ride broke down.

LANA MITCHELL ◆ MECHANICSBURG, PA

....

MY SONS MARTY AND PATRICK grew up in Los Angeles and were ardent UCLA Bruins fans. We'd center our winter vacation around the team's bowl appearances. We followed the Bruins to the Alamo Bowl, to the Las Vegas Bowl, and to bowls in San Jose, San Diego and San Francisco.

The boys anticipated bowl games almost as much as Christmas. In fact, their letters to Santa almost always included requests for UCLA T-shirts and hoodies.

LISA SHERIDAN ◆ CINCINNATI, OH

Jane looks every inch the Razorback fan as she gets ready for the 1966 Cotton Bowl.

Lost in a Fog

A heartbreaking travel delay ends up being for the best.

JANE GATEWOOD ◆ RECTOR, AR

When the Arkansas Razorbacks made it into the 1966 Cotton Bowl against Louisiana State University, a trip to Dallas, Texas, would become my Christmas and birthday presents wrapped into one.

My family gave me a color-coordinated skirt, blazer, purse and heels, plus a set of red luggage. A vision in Razorback red and white, I suited up for the game. But a call came early on New Year's Day that Dallas Love Field was socked in with rain and fog—our airplane was grounded.

The bowl game turned out badly, too. Jon Brittenum, the Arkansas quarterback, suffered a shoulder injury, and then the Razorbacks lost 14-7. I cried when our flight was canceled, but I'm glad I was not in the stadium to witness such a heartbreaking loss.

A Rewarding Night for a Racing Fan

A night at the race track took an unexpected turn.

PAT ANGELL LEIVE ◆ KANSAS CITY, MO

Where do daredevil drivers start their romance with speed? Olympic Stadium in Kansas City, Missouri, was one such place. The ⅕-mile dirt track brought drivers from distant cities, some of whom became big names in racing. A guy from Texas named A.J. Foyt scored his first-ever United States Auto Club win at Olympic Stadium on May 12, 1957. He went on to win the Indianapolis 500 four times and was inducted into the International Motorsports Hall of Fame in 2000.

My parents were devoted fans of the Sunday night races at Olympic Stadium. One summer night in 1950, wearing my new cotton strapless dress, I went with them to the races. Much to my surprise, a race organizer asked me to award the trophy to the winner of the big race. I was chauffeured around the track in an open convertible, then I presented the cup to the unexpected winner, James Campbell. He was a race car owner, but he'd had to take the wheel himself that night when his driver failed to show up. After that win, Campbell became a premier racer on the International Motor Contest Association circuit.

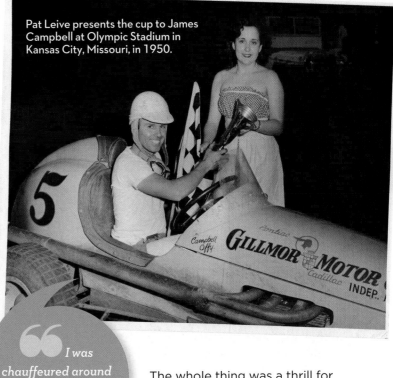

Pat Leive presents the cup to James Campbell at Olympic Stadium in Kansas City, Missouri, in 1950.

> *I was chauffeured around the track in an open convertible...*

The whole thing was a thrill for a young girl. A few weeks later I left for college and so didn't get another chance that summer to present the winning trophy at a race.

I still reflect on those long-gone days at Olympic Stadium. The memories of that time always bring a smile to my face and hold a very special place in my heart.

TEEING UP

CARL VINCENT of Medical Lake, Washington, found this image of a female golfer in his uncle John Court's slide collection. A golf fan, John took dozens of pictures of pro and amateur players during the 1950s.

In Daytona, at the Corner of Beach and Asphalt

He manned the radio as cars whizzed by. **JOHN S. "JACK" GIBSON** ◆ HIDEAWAY, TX

While a college student in 1953, I volunteered at the Daytona Beach, Florida, raceway to help with the radio communications for the Daytona Beach Road Course.

As the name suggests, the sandy beach made up one half of the 4.2-mile circuit and a parallel asphalt two-lane road the other half. The turns were banked curves of hard, packed sand.

I was one of several licensed amateur radio operators stationed at points along the route. Our job was to let the public address announcer know which car was in the lead and report on any accidents. I was assigned to the north turn near the grandstand, where the course went from beach to paved road. The green flag dropped at the south turn.

We were told it was the first time the race had used modern radio communications. Before that they'd used a phone line between the north and south ends of the course—primitive and unreliable. I still have the 1953 NASCAR announcer armband I wore as a race volunteer.

My most vivid memory from those two days of racing is of the cars approaching the north turn at the start of the first race. So many were bunched together that there simply wasn't room for all of them. Several cars literally flew over the curved, banked edge to tumble and roll in the soft sand below.

Drivers compete in a classic race at Daytona Beach, Florida. Jack's armband (top left) identified him as a radio communications volunteer.

Still Indy After All These Years

It took only one race to hook them for years to come.

RICHARD STONE ◆ NORTH TONAWANDA, NY

My buddy Tom Burns and I took off in 1965 in my 3-month-old '65 Corvette for our first trip to the Indianapolis 500.

We couldn't believe that the race cars, at the time, were doing almost 160 mph. My eyes popped out of my head. I was hooked on Indy.

I would go with various friends every year until 1970, when my new wife, Linda, went with me— and then she was hooked on Indy, too.

One year she made us and two of our friends matching pants that looked like the checkered flag. We were a hit in those pants! Everyone loved them.

We've gone every year and sat in the same seats since 1976. We've seen some wonderful times, great races and many famous drivers, including Mario Andretti, Al Unser Sr. and Jr., and A.J. Foyt. We were there in 1985 when Danny Sullivan made his famous "spin-and-win," spinning 360 degrees on a turn to lose the lead, then a few laps later going on to beat front-runner Andretti.

We've been to the race on days when it was beautiful and on days when it rained, when it was 95 degrees and when it was 55 degrees with the wind blowing like crazy.

We've never missed a race. In the spring, we start counting down until race day. Boy, do we love that Indy 500!

Richard kept all of his Indy tickets over the years. Many of them are autographed by race winners.

Don Larsen's perfect game in 1956 was the first ever in a World Series. There hasn't been one since. The Yankees went on to win the series in Game 7, thumping the Dodgers 9-0.

Perfect Day for a Perfect Game

The 2016 World Series also marked the 60th anniversary of Don Larsen's perfect game. I was a senior at Nutley High School in New Jersey in 1956, and I have fond memories of that glorious October afternoon.

Back then, New York baseball, consisting of the Yankees, Dodgers and Giants, was the very best on the planet. No matter which team you rooted for, you had a strong chance to enjoy bragging rights.

In Game 5 of the 1956 World Series, the New York Yankees were playing their rivals, the Brooklyn Dodgers, at Yankee Stadium. Not only did the Yankees' pitcher Don Larsen have a no-hitter going, but he also had a perfect game in the works.

The halls and classrooms of school were abuzz with the news. When classes ended for the day,

those of us on the football team headed down to the locker room. As we trickled through the door in twos and threes, we found our coaches, Sandy Phillips, Ed Deitch, Lou Zwirek and Ralph D'Andrea, huddled around the radio.

On any other day, they would have been scurrying about the locker room exhorting players to get into their practice uniforms and start running laps. But not that day.

On that day, there was a sense that history was about to be made. And all of us wanted to be a part of it.

It was the top of the ninth inning, with two out. Brooklyn's Dale Mitchell, a .312 lifetime hitter, was batting. Announcer Bob Wolff called the play-by-play: "Larsen is ready, gets the sign—two strikes, one ball. Here comes the pitch. Strike three! A no-hitter, a perfect game for Don Larsen!"

OUT 2

The New York Yankees celebrate another World Series victory at Ebbets Field in 1956 (below). Mickey Mantle (bottom) hits a thrilling homer in the fourth inning of Game 5.

296

WITH A WINK AND A NOD

ON A TRIP WITH MY DAD to Shibe Park in Philadelphia to watch my beloved Athletics in the summer of 1949, my real purpose in going was to see Ted Williams play for the first time.

I followed Ted in the box scores every day. It seemed to me, at 7 years old, that Ted always had two or three hits every time I looked. After checking Ted's statistics, I always peeked at my team, the Athletics. Most of the time, they registered another defeat.

As we settled into our seats behind the Boston Red Sox dugout to watch batting practice, my heart raced while I looked in all directions for number 9, Ted Williams. There he was in the outfield playing catch with his buddy Johnny Pesky.

Soon, he started walking toward the infield for batting practice and went to the plate to hit. Crack! Crack! Bang! Bang! The balls hit the right field wall. His line drives were loud and sounded like a cannon shot.

Then my dad, always a leather lung, prodded me to stand up as Ted walked toward us in our seats about eight rows behind the dugout. "Hey, Ted!" yelled my dad, loud enough for the whole park to hear. Ted looked up quickly, right at me, and winked.

I was on cloud nine. I had never been more thankful for my dad's booming voice. Wow! Ted Williams actually winked at me.

WILLIAM BARNA ◆ SLATINGTON, PA

The locker room erupted with cheers and curses. Immediately, the coaches became coaches again, doing what all coaches do, saying: "C'mon, guys, fun's over. Let's get out there, we've got work to do."

We would have to wait until we got home to watch the evening news and see the now-iconic footage of catcher Yogi Berra leaping into Larsen's arms after the Yankees' 2-0 victory. History was indeed made that day.

DICK NEUBERT ◆ NUTLEY, NJ

Little League players stand together at a game.

Outfielder's Gaffe Soon Forgotten

Despite player's big mental error, his team pulled off a miraculous win.

FRANK J. GAGLIARDI • MILLBURY, MA

The year was 1956. I was 12 and playing right field for the Little League Championship in my hometown of Millbury, Massachusetts. The game was scoreless in the top of the last inning with two outs. A batter on the other team lined a base hit to me in the outfield.

Against everything I'd ever been taught and over the screams of our coach to throw the ball to second, I committed the cardinal sin of all baseball sins and threw the ball to first base. The ball and the runner arrived at the base at the same time, and all I could see were hats and gloves and bodies flying everywhere.

While the umpires and coaches gathered together and tried to sort out what had happened, I wanted to dig a hole in the outfield

GAME: COURTESY OF LITTLE LEAGUE BASEBALL AND SOFTBALL

CHECK OUT MY TICKET STUB

MY HUSBAND, GORDON, has been a die-hard Dodger fan since the team moved to Los Angeles in October 1957 when he was 8 years old.

On our first date, when he found out I liked baseball, he opened his wallet and pulled out a ticket stub to Sandy Koufax's perfect game—he still has it!

He and his mom attended the game on Sept. 9, 1965, when Gordon was 15. They had box seats on the third base side, and they were on the edge of their seats the whole game. His mom was so nervous that she chewed her nails down.

Gordon now says it was the most exciting game of his life.

CHRIS MICHALSKI HUGO
SPRINGFIELD, OR

Sandy Koufax, the Dodgers' impressive lefty, pitched a perfect game against the Chicago Cubs in Dodger Stadium, Los Angeles, in 1965. The Dodgers claimed a 1-0 victory.

and climb into it. I was sure I had cost my team the championship.

Then the umpires made a ruling that surely pleased one team and outraged the other—declaring the runner out for interfering with a fielder trying to catch a ball.

When we all ran off the field, I stood as far from my teammates as possible, sure that they wanted to throw me off the team. Suddenly there was a loud roar, and I looked up to see our best hitter line a home run over the center-field fence to win the game for us, 1-0.

My mistake was forgotten as we mobbed our teammate at home plate. To top it all off, we headed to our after-game spot, the local dairy bar, for ice cream.

Is it last week's game? Or tonight's?

Zenith's new Video Cassette Recorder. For a picture so good it's hard to tell from the original program.

If you're about to buy a video cassette recorder, buy one that gives you superb picture quality. The kind of picture quality that Zenith is famous for.
Get the convenience features you've been looking for, too. Like built-in tuner and automatic timer. So you can record shows while you're watching something on another channel or even when you're not at home. And don't forget a remote pause control.
Buy a video cassette recorder that gives you all of the above.
The convenience features you want plus the picture quality and reliability you'd expect. All from Zenith.

ZENITH
The quality goes in before the name goes on.®

MODEL KR9000W Video Cassette Recorder with cabinet of simulated wood finish. Simulated television picture.

1978

THIS ZENITH AD, which ran in *Time*, came a mere three years after Sony introduced the VCR to the world—and the device was already a hot commodity. By 1984, one in seven U.S. households would own a VCR. Zenith justified its higher prices by emphasizing its slogan, "The quality goes in before the name goes on."

A Bad Moment, Bar None

A teammate's prank embarrasses, but one article of clothing manages to save the day.

MARK CHRISTENSON • COLUMBIA HEIGHTS, MN

During junior high and high school, from 1961 to 1967, in Albert Lea, Minnesota, I was part of the gymnastics team. We shared our practice facility, a junior high gymnasium, with the pompom girls.

> "Some laughed, some looked shocked, and some frowned and looked away. But all of them saw me."

Our coach, Vern Arndt, insisted that everyone on his team (known as "Arndt's monkeys") wear jockstraps. He also insisted that whatever your specialty, every team member had to practice on every piece of equipment. I was a tumbler and free-exercise man, but I tried my best to work with the other apparatus, too.

One day, when I was about 15, as the pompom girls were practicing their routines on the other side of the gym, I jumped up and grabbed the high bar. I was using absolutely perfect form, straight body, feet pointing to the ground.

Suddenly, another gymnast snuck up behind me and pulled my gym shorts down to my ankles. I was in utter shock. I clung to the high bar, unable to let go. The pompom girls had mixed reactions to my situation. Some laughed, some looked shocked, and some frowned and looked away. But all of them saw me.

Finally, I managed to drop from the bar and run to the locker room. I threatened to quit the team but Coach Arndt talked me out of it.

Looking back on that day, I am thankful for only one thing: the jockstrap.

Applause for a One-Handed Catch

An amazing catch gets young boy a moment with famous baseball player.

STEVE SHARP ◆ OVILLA, TX

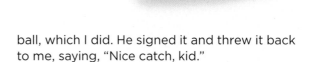

My neighbor invited me, as an eighth-grader from Crawfordsville, Indiana, to join him, his brothers and his father on a trip to Chicago's Wrigley Field to watch the Cubs play the San Francisco Giants. We had great seats, about eight rows up from the field past first base on the right field line.

We had just finished our Little League season, so we naturally took our gloves with us in hopes of catching that elusive foul ball. Willie McCovey, the Giants first baseman, was at bat. He ripped a line-drive foul ball so fast that I just held up my glove and caught it as if I were playing catch. To my surprise, applause erupted, and a few minutes later McCovey came up to the fence and asked where the boy was who caught his ball. I raised my hand. He asked me to toss him the

ball, which I did. He signed it and threw it back to me, saying, "Nice catch, kid."

I played baseball all the way through college but never received an applause like the one I got at Wrigley that July afternoon in 1965.

It was awesome to watch the likes of McCovey, Willie Mays and Ernie Banks that summer day. The sad thing is, this was before I knew that autograph would be worth something. So I went out the very next day and played ball in the backyard with my signed McCovey ball.

ON THE SQUAD

SHIRLEY BOWMAN (right) was a song leader for Biola College in La Mirada, California, in the early 1960s. Fifty years later, her uniform still fits, according to her husband, Howard, of Duncanville, Texas.

OLD-SCHOOL FOOTBALL

THIS IS BILLY JOE PETTY when he was a junior and on the starting line for the McKinney High School Lions football team in 1946. "Players in those days did double duty, working both offense and defense, with almost no chance to rest," says DeWayne Owens of McKinney, Texas. "Face masks didn't exist, so broken noses and busted lips were common."

SUITABLE FOR SKIING

LYNN POLSON'S GRANDFATHER Hans and his neighbor, Henry Loebsack, built the first ski-hill towrope in the Waterville, Washington, area. In the photo, Lynn's father, Elton, skis with friend Lucille Loebsack.

HE PLAYED HARD

ROBERT GAMELIN (No. 9, second row) didn't know he'd punctured a kidney on a block while playing tight end for Winooski (Vermont) High School in 1952. "The career-ending injury put me in the hospital for seven weeks."

BATTER UP!

GROWING UP in east-central Minnesota, Will Hubin of Kent, Ohio, had an empty lot in the back of his house complete with its own backstop. In this photo, Will's older brother Al takes a mighty swing.

CHAMPS FOR THE YEAR

NO FUTURE HALL OF FAMERS, these kids just loved to play baseball, including Richard Dvorak, now of Charlotte, North Carolina. The team was from Queens, New York, and they were the 1952 champs of the Long Island City YMCA Novice Traveling Division.

MASPETH PHILLIES-L.I.C. YMCA CHAMPS
~ NOVICE TRAVELING DIVISION - 1952 ~
ANDING - KOSIOR, MICHAL, BRANDON, MULLER, MORRIS, DVORAK, MONTEVERSE, MORAN
TTING - CAJDARIK, SANTUCCI, B. KANE, MGR; VECCHIONE, ZEHNTER÷FRONT, RATH

Saint Teresa's Baseball Team of 1945.

TEAM PHOTO TIME

TAKEN IN 1945, this classic portrait shows the St. Teresa's baseball team of North Tarrytown, New York. Father Frey was the team's coach, and standing over his right shoulder is Joseph R. Murray, father-in-law of James Moneymaker of Menands, New York. James tells us Joe is about 13 and in the seventh grade here.

Boxing Gloves Traded for Driving Gloves

Dad's youthful connections were rekindled years later.

BRUCE DEVUE TAVEY ◆ REDDING, CA

One thing in life you have no say about is your name. Born during the Great Depression on April 14, 1932, I got my first name from my father. He named me after his childhood friend Bruce Dempsey, younger brother of the great heavyweight boxer Jack Dempsey.

Jack got his start at Peter Jackson's Saloon in Salt Lake City, Utah, which had a working gym. My father lived two blocks from the gym as a young boy. He and Bruce hung around the place and did small chores for tips.

Dad later became a boxer, working in Jack's stable, fighting in the oil and mining towns in Utah, Nevada, Wyoming and Colorado. After I was born, Jack knew my dad wanted to get back to his family in Salt Lake, so he bought a big car in Denver and hired Dad as the Dempsey family chauffeur in Salt Lake City.

Dad's mother, my Grandma Tavey, was a housekeeper for Jack's folks as well. The family joke was that Mrs. Dempsey would have Dad pick Mom and me and Grandma up in the big car on Sundays and drive us sightseeing in the canyons.

We moved to California during WWII and lost track of our friends the Dempseys. Eventually, I joined the Navy and became a chief reactor operator on a nuclear submarine.

In 1962, after I returned to New London, Connecticut, from a mission, Mom and Dad came to visit. We went to a show in New York City and afterward to Jack Dempsey's Restaurant. I told the maître d' that my dad knew Jack from the old days, and 30 minutes later, Jack came to our table. He and my dad talked for two hours. I've never seen my dad so thrilled.

Jack Dempsey delivers a knockdown punch to Jess Willard in their heavyweight title match in 1919.

66 *My son Ronald played hockey from age 14 up through his 40s—and he has the scars to prove it! Here he's at center front, posing with his Mayville, Wisconsin, team in 1956.* 99

HOLLY SCHROEDER • NORTH FOND DU LAC, WI

BRUSHES WITH FAME

Chance encounters with stars from the big screen, music, television, politics and more result in bragging rights for years to come.

CHAPTER 9

So Near and Now So Far

He passed up the opportunity to shake a future president's hand. **BOB McILHENNY** • SAN DIEGO, CA

Back in 1960, I was going to school in Chicago and had a part-time job with a catering company, too. On Sept. 26, 1960, I was working the banquet where Sen. John F. Kennedy was to speak after his first debate with Vice President Richard M. Nixon. The banquet was a full sit-down dinner, and it was packed.

As both a Republican and a Protestant, I was not a Kennedy fan. Indeed, I'm sorry to say that I was quite the opposite.

So I don't know why I pushed to get to the front of the greeters when Kennedy arrived. But there I was in line to shake his hand. He was moving closer, and I was determined not to shake his hand or even to look into his face. I recall this decision with great regret today. I do remember the questions he asked the waitresses standing on either side of me: "Is everyone well in your family? Does your husband have a steady job? Do you feel your children are getting a good education?" He was so personable, I wondered at the time if he actually knew them.

Later that evening, he gave a speech that seemed to hypnotize his audience. Cheers, laughter, silence—whatever the senator wanted from the crowd was exactly what he got.

Oh, how neat it would have been for me—a future teacher of American history—to be able to say that I had met and shaken hands with John Kennedy. But I can't.

I did learn a valuable lesson, though: Don't allow a personal prejudice to keep you from doing something you may regret. *Carpe diem!*

Enthusiastic supporters (bottom left) applaud Sen. John Kennedy's campaign arrival in Columbus, Ohio, in October 1960. Earlier that month, Kennedy greets a roadside crowd in Indiana, below.

Privy to Her Prized Possessions

You never know what you'll come across when moving other people's belongings.

FRANK E. MORRISON • GARDEN GROVE, CA

After I graduated from high school in the late '60s, I became a mover. As I learned the trade and gained knowledge of the industry, I relocated from Chicago, Illinois, to Southern California, where I worked for a United Van Lines agency.

On a beautiful day in July 1970, I was assigned to pack the belongings of a pretty important person: Claire Trevor, the movie star. And what a beautiful, amazing lady she was.

She sat with me and showed me backstage photos of stars such as Ronald Reagan, Humphrey Bogart, Lauren Bacall, Howard Hughes and the Duke, John Wayne.

Then I did something that I'll cherish forever, and that not many people can say they've done. I held an Oscar in one hand and an Emmy in the other. Claire Trevor won the Best Supporting Actress Oscar in 1949 for her role in *Key Largo* with Humphrey Bogart and Edward G. Robinson, and her Emmy for a *Producers' Showcase* episode titled "Dodsworth" in '57.

On the day we loaded the furniture into the moving van, John Wayne came to her house to say goodbye. He brought a six-pack of beer for the movers and shot the breeze with us for more than an hour.

During my 38 years in the moving business, I have met 14 movie stars and one president. But when I think about my three days with Claire Trevor, I still get goose bumps.

FUN FACTS

CLAIRE TREVOR was born Claire Wemlinger on March 8, 1910, in Brooklyn, New York.

• •

NICKNAMED the Queen of Film Noir.

• •

STAR OF stage, radio, television and film.

• •

HAD A CAREER spanning seven decades and appearances in more than 60 films.

• •

NOMINATED for three Best Supporting Actress Oscars.

• •

NOMINATED for two Best Actress Emmy awards.

Good girl gone bad, gun molls and a washed-up nightclub singer were a few of the roles that Claire Trevor stamped with her distinctive voice and range of emotions.

Who Cares About McCarthy?!

In the spring of 1968, Janice, Pauline and I worked at the local newspaper in Manitowoc, Wisconsin. One day we heard from one of our news reporters that the actor Paul Newman would be in town campaigning for Democratic candidate Sen. Eugene McCarthy.

My friends and I were not into politics; we barely knew who McCarthy was, but we sure knew who Paul Newman was! We raced to the Mid-Cities Mall in downtown Manitowoc in my friend's Dodge Dart. Once there, we saw the McCarthy sign atop the car carrying Newman, so we ran over to it and rushed to get as close as we could.

I can still remember Newman's positively blue eyes. I even got to touch his sleeve! Of course,

our entire afternoon at work was nothing but chatter and excitement over standing so close to a movie star.

Later that afternoon, the newspaper's photographer told us he would get us all a picture of the event. All these years later and usually during a presidential election year, I still reminisce about that day.

JULIE KREIL ◆ TWO RIVERS, WI

Julie (top right in a fur-collared coat) was a mere step away from movie star Paul Newman during a campaign stop for Sen. Eugene McCarthy in 1968. Also pictured are Julie's friends Janice (at rear with her hand on Julie's shoulder) and Pauline (black bob haircut and dark coat).

> *I can still remember Newman's positively blue eyes. I even got to touch his sleeve!*

MY SHOOT-OUT WITH TONTO occurred in a Menlo Park, California, supermarket parking lot. *The Lone Ranger* was my favorite show, so when the traveling show came to town, I went in my cowboy boots and hat, packing two six-guns. I got picked for the quick-draw contest against Tonto, and he let me win. At the end of the show, Tonto gave me two autographed pictures. Best day ever!

ALVIN DEXTER ◆ POLLOCK PINES, CA

1953

Now Millions Know! ONE
KING SIZE
tops 'em all for TASTE and COMFORT!

*Your throat can tell...
its PHILIP MORRIS*

KING-SIZE

REGULAR

CALL FOR **PHILIP MORRIS**

I LOVE LUCY was No. 1 in the ratings in four of its six seasons, and show sponsor Philip Morris saw its stock rise right along with it. Lucille Ball's striking red hair and blue eyes pop off the page here—a shock, most likely, to anyone used to seeing the star in only black-and-white on a tiny TV screen.

On the Good Ship Shirley Temple

My husband, Freddie Groen, was a photojournalist for a local TV station in northern Illinois. Occasionally I would be asked to cover a story to air on the news.

In 1968, I took a last-minute call to cover a fundraising dinner for the Republican candidate, Richard Nixon. I was to interview the guest speaker before the event. The station manager told me it was Mrs. Shirley Black. I didn't know who that was, but when I got to the event someone gave me a list of questions to ask her.

While the cameras and audio were being set up I looked over the questions, most of which were about her political aspirations. But one of them was, "Do you feel you have more influence in your campaigning because you were a child star?" I still had no idea who I would be interviewing.

All of a sudden, Mrs. Black came into sight and I just about fainted. When I realized I was about to interview Shirley Temple, the former child movie star, I lost all focus and couldn't find any words. My mind went blank and I stuttered, which I didn't normally do.

She was an absolute delight and eased my fears with a few words.

"Honey," Shirley Temple Black said, "just talk to me like you would your mama."

The interview went off without a hitch, and she hugged me as she left.

I voted for Nixon that year even though I probably wouldn't have even voted if it hadn't been for my good luck meeting Shirley Temple. As history would have it, I guess my choice for president wasn't the smartest, but I am a diehard Shirley Temple fan to this day.

CAROL MAUST ◆ HOUSTON, TX

Carol's husband, Freddie, snapped this picture of her interviewing Shirley Temple Black (left) during the 1968 Nixon presidential campaign.

A Trudeau, Then and Now

Her husband helped her meet a prime minister. **JANETTE BURNHAM LOZON** ◆ TROUT LAKE, MI

As a Canadian I've been privileged to see three prime ministers in person. But the most memorable was when I shook hands with Pierre Elliott Trudeau during his 1980 election campaign.

In May 1979, Progressive Conservative Joe Clark became prime minister when his party beat the Liberals under Mr. Trudeau, who had governed the country for 11 years. A few months later, Mr. Trudeau announced his intention to retire from public life.

Before this happened, though, the Conservative government brought down an austerity budget that included a gas tax of 18 cents per gallon, which upset a lot of Canadians. The budget was defeated in the House of Commons, and then Joe Clark's minority government was thrown out of power after only nine months.

The Liberals persuaded Pierre Trudeau to stay on and run in the Feb. 8, 1980, election. My husband, Ray, and I volunteered for the campaign, and we were thrilled when Pierre Trudeau made a campaign stop at the county seat in Chatham, Ontario, which was not far from where we lived.

He was making his way through the crowd, smiling, nodding and occasionally shaking hands. Although I was close, I was too shy to reach out to him. But when Mr. Trudeau was almost parallel to me, I suddenly felt my husband's hand on my elbow. He thrust my arm forward, right into Mr. Trudeau's path. The candidate stopped, shook my hand, looked me in the eye and smiled a greeting. I'll never forget those blue eyes and the straightforward way he looked at me.

The Liberals won a resounding majority in 1980. That was the only election Ray and I ever worked on, but we cheered enthusiastically from the sidelines in 2015 when Pierre Trudeau's son Justin Trudeau led the Liberals to a landslide victory to become Canada's 23rd prime minister.

Maybe someday I'll shake his hand, too.

Canada's then-Prime Minister Pierre Elliott Trudeau visits the Acropolis in Greece in 1980 with his sons, Michel (left), Justin (rear) and Alexandre, called Sasha. In 2015 Justin Trudeau (lower left) became Canada's 23rd prime minister.

At a golf benefit in Los Angeles, California, Laura and her husband, Cy Harrington (far right), rub elbows with (from left) Mary Pickford's husband, Buddy Rogers, and screenwriter Ali Ipar.

Traveling with the Stars

Her work for a Hollywood film icon gave her a front-row seat.

LaVON MARSHALL ◆ SALT LAKE CITY, UT

When my great-aunt Laura LaFranchi attended Manual Arts High School in Los Angeles, California, she made it her goal to work for an important man. Several years later, her dream became a reality when Twentieth Century-Fox co-founder Darryl F. Zanuck hired her as his secretary in the 1940s. He had begun working on the film *Laura* and was intrigued that my great-aunt had the same name.

For Laura, the next 19 years were a whirlwind of travel to Fox studios in Rome, Paris and New York City. She went on location for Zanuck's movies and traveled with the family to Sun Valley, Idaho. There, she borrowed ice skating attire from Sonja Henie, the Norwegian figure skater, and golfed with celebrities such as Bing Crosby, Ronald Reagan and Jane Wyman, and Bob and Dolores Hope.

While on location for *The Sun Also Rises*, Laura became acquainted with Audrey Hepburn, who was there to join her husband Mel Ferrer, one of the movie's stars. Laura recalled how down-to-earth Hepburn was as they sat together while the actress, her hair pulled back in pigtails, peeled oranges for everyone on set to enjoy. When Hepburn hosted a birthday party for Eddie Albert, she invited Laura to attend.

Other celebrities Laura mingled with included Errol Flynn, Robert Evans and Truman Capote. Once, after Zanuck and Laura watched Judy Garland perform onstage in New York City, Zanuck took Laura and a few other celebrities to meet Garland at El Morocco, a nightclub frequented by the rich and famous.

One of the highlights of my great-aunt's life was attending the London premiere in 1962 of *The Longest Day*, a Hollywood epic and eventual winner of the 1963 Academy Awards for the best black-and-white cinematography and special effects. Laura and her husband had seats in the queen's royal box.

A month before she died, my great-aunt shared stories with my sister and me about her exploits. She had kept articles and news clippings for decades attesting to the fact that dreams really can come true.

A Stage Away from Heaven

Joe Smith and I were in the 11th grade in 1975 when we got tickets to Led Zeppelin at the Tarrant County Convention Center in Fort Worth, Texas. I had just turned 17.

We were on the floor, about 100 feet from the band. Just before the encore started, I got out of my seat and made my way to the stage, which had no barrier to keep the crowd back. Zeppelin came on again and went into "Whole Lotta Love," a hard-driving song with a fantastic lead solo toward the end.

Suddenly the guitarist, Jimmy Page, leaped forward and slid on his knees to where I was standing. He let rip with his blistering solo right before my eyes. *Wow,* I was thinking, *this is amazing!*

I saw Led Zeppelin again in 1977, but I will never forget that moment of being inches from a rock legend.

STEPHEN SMITH ◆ TERRELL, TX

> " *He let rip with his blistering solo right before my eyes.* "

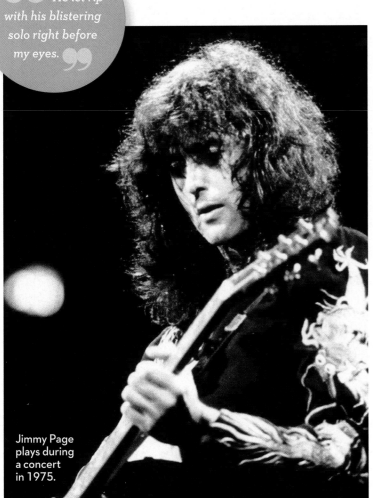

Jimmy Page plays during a concert in 1975.

BARRY PEAKE/SHUTTERSTOCK

CHARLES LAUGHTON had won his only Academy Award back in 1934, but he was enjoying a career resurgence in the late 1940s, with prominent character roles in *The Big Clock* (1948), and *The Bribe* and *The Man on the Eiffel Tower* (both 1949). With his posh English accent and theatrical demeanor, Laughton wasn't an obvious fit for the Pabst brand, but that seems to be the point. "Our beer is so good," the ad is saying, "even this fancy British guy drinks it."

Uncle Dennis Knew His Way Around Taylor Street

Life in Chicago's Little Italy neighborhood inspired one famous detective's acting career. **FRANK E. MORRISON** • GARDEN GROVE, CA

When I was growing up in the heart of Chicago's famous Italian neighborhood on Taylor Street, everyone was like family. Neighbors sat on their front porches, visiting and talking for hours.

When I was in fourth grade, Dennis Farina was a Chicago police detective. He would pull up in front of our house, walk into the kitchen and come out eating a bowl of my mother's meat loaf. To us, he was Uncle Dennis, a great guy who was always there for you.

Dennis Farina left the police force in 1985, after the producer Michael Mann hired him for a lead role in his new TV series, *Crime Story.* Uncle Dennis went on to a successful career in both movies and television.

Years later I was in Los Angeles at the opening of *Get Shorty* (1995). Dennis Farina and the rest of the cast were there, shaking hands and talking to fans. When I approached Dennis, I asked if he had any memories of Taylor Street. He shot back with my nickname, Butch, and told me that he still yearned for a bowl of my mom's meat loaf. I was amazed and got chills up my back.

As I was leaving, I was stopped by theater security and they ushered me to the VIP box. I sat with John Travolta and Danny DeVito. Uncle Dennis and I laughed and talked through the whole movie about our memorable times on Taylor Street. He died in 2013, but what an outstanding man he was. It was a golden day I'll take to my grave. There aren't too many left like Uncle Dennis.

Farina began his acting career when he was 37.

MARKA/ALAMY STOCK PHOTO

An Afternoon with the Duke

Kindness leaves a lasting impression.

LINDA L. SHOOK ◆ LAKEWOOD, WA

One cold morning in March 1955, my parents decided to take a road trip from our rural farm in Tacoma, Washington, to Southern California. We went to visit my dad's family—my grandfather, uncles, aunts and cousins. My mom and dad left the farm in the hands of the neighbors and, along with my brother, 5, and my grandma, we all piled into the car and headed south on Old 99.

I don't remember how many days we traveled, but I remember being annoyed by my younger brother even before we hit the Oregon border. There was constant seat switching so we could both survive the miles. I was upset because I knew Disneyland wasn't opening until July, and I couldn't understand why my parents wouldn't wait to take this trip.

Once we got to California, we spent a day at Knott's Berry Farm and Olvera Street (the historic market). Then one day my Uncle Don, a freelance photographer for the movie studios, invited me to spend a day at work with him. My parents agreed. So they took me to the Hollywood Robert Hall store, where I got a new outfit, and the next morning Uncle Don picked me up. I was nervous but excited, especially when he said I was going to meet a couple of movie stars.

When we got to the studio, a scene was being shot, and everything was quiet. How thrilling. At lunch, Uncle Don took me to meet the stars— Lauren Bacall and John Wayne. They were shooting a scene for the movie *Blood Alley*.

Lauren Bacall sat for a photo and then walked away. But John Wayne was amazing. He was engaging and kind to this shy 13-year-old farm girl from western Washington. We took pictures and had lunch just off the set. Then my uncle took me back to my parents.

All the scuffling with my little brother on that long road trip was worth it to get to meet one of the all-time greats. The Duke will always be my hero.

Getting her photo taken with real-life celebrity John Wayne dissolved any problems Linda had with her little brother.

1957

New kind of pen even fills itself by itself—this new way

This man has received a unique gift . . . and he's watching something revolutionary happen. It's a new Parker 61 literally drinking up ink all by itself by capillary "suction." He has simply removed the barrel cover, and set the pen in the ink upside down. It fills full in seconds.

Now he'll lift the Parker 61 from the ink. No wiping needed because ink can't cling to the special barrel surface. This entirely new filling method is just one among many wonders of the Parker 61. It's virtually shockproof. Due to viewing parts to get out of order. The ink supply is over-visible. Writes cleanly, clearly, smoothly even when held point up, or when high in air either. The classic beauty of the Parker 61, the distinctive colors, the gleaming caps of precious metals—all make this pen a most discriminating choice for Christmas giving. The Parker 61 Capillary Pen is $20.00 or more. Visit your Parker Franchised Dealer.

Parker 61
Capillary Pen

Unlike any other gift in this world

THE AD NEVER IDENTIFIES
Bob Hope, referring only to "this man," but in 1957, there was no mistaking him. Perhaps America's best-known comedian, Hope was a fixture on TV at the time. Parker likely paid top dollar for his endorsement. No wonder it had to charge $20 (about $172 today) for its Capillary Pen.

She Found Her Place in the Falling Turf

The all-day rain crushed my romantic notions of the outdoor summer concert. No barely clothed bodies gyrating in the summer sun for us. Instead, we were layered in hoodies, wet denim and soggy shoes. I was 16, and this was Lollapalooza at Great Woods, a vast open-air venue in Mansfield, Massachusetts, in 1991.

When Nine Inch Nails played "Head like a Hole," the crowd started to rip up chunks of grass and hurl them into the air. The sky was raining clumps of mud and turf, and the ground had become a brown swamp.

I can't remember exactly who I was there with. I'm 80 percent sure it was Rob Devaney, the stage-combat teacher at my summer theater school. I had come to see Jane's Addiction, which was on permanent rotation in my personal remix that year. It appealed to my inky well of adolescent despair and rage.

Heads thrashed as Living Colour ground out "Cult of Personality." I saw a girl in a black miniskirt and platform boots, mascara running down her cheeks, slumped and sagging almost on the ground, too sick to stand.

Siouxsie Sioux's sultry voice carried the crowd toward twilight and Jane's Addiction. The bass rumbled on a black stage for what felt like forever, and when the headliner finally came on, the crowd was ablaze.

Damp and muddy, we twisted and wrenched in reaction to Perry Farrell's growl and wail. The people in front of us, the ones in the mosh pit, were like painted brutes in the near dark, ramming each other and convulsing in unison. I stood bewitched, allured by the mood, the music and a sick nervous anticipation for what was to come.

LAURA ELIZABETH WOOD • GREENWOOD LAKE, NY

At 16, Laura saw her spiritual muse, Perry Farrell of Jane's Addiction, at the Lollapalooza concert in Great Woods in 1991.

Catching a Star's Campaign Pitch

My greatest thrill as a St. Louis Cardinals fan came during a campaign rally for John Kennedy in Omaha, Nebraska, in early fall 1960.

I was stationed at Strategic Air Command headquarters when my staff sergeant heard that Stanley "Stan The Man" Musial, the great star hitter for the Cardinals, was going to be at the Omaha rally.

We arrived, parked the car and walked into an area where coffee and doughnuts were being served. Musial wasn't there, although we did see Ted Kennedy's wife, Joan; writer James Michener, who was talking about his novel *Hawaii*; and the actors Jeff Chandler and Angie Dickinson.

> " *A convertible pulled up and, sure enough, there in the passenger seat was Stan Musial.* "

After about 15 minutes we went back outside. A convertible pulled up and, sure enough, there in the passenger seat was Stan Musial. We made a beeline for him and shook his hand, telling him we were big fans.

"Well, boys," he said, "get in the backseat and let's talk some baseball."

I could not believe it! For the next 30 minutes, while the campaign speakers talked about Kennedy's chances for the presidency, we talked with Stan Musial about the Cardinals' chances for the pennant.

I did manage to get signatures from all the famous campaigners, including Stan's, on a brochure, but unfortunately, my mother, not realizing what it was, threw the brochure away some years later.

LEON FREEMAN ◆ MOKENA, IL

St. Louis Cardinals slugger Stan Musial, his wife, Lillian, and daughter Janet, visit President Kennedy at the White House in July 1962.

The Marilyn We Knew

One of Dave Ketchum's and my assignments in the radio and TV section of the public information office at Camp Roberts, California, in 1952 was to write, produce and perform a weekly half-hour radio show that aired over KPRL in Paso Robles and other stations near the camp.

Part of the show consisted of a taped interview with a popular movie star, usually selected by our listeners, who included some of the 40,000 troops undergoing infantry training at Camp Roberts. Marilyn Monroe was always the number one choice of the GIs.

We finally got a chance to interview her at the 20th Century-Fox studios in Los Angeles, about 250 miles south. The studio publicist warned us that the actress was gaining a reputation for being late and, sometimes, uncooperative. We were undeterred. Dave did the interview—he'd had his own radio show in San Diego before he was called to active duty in the Army. I operated the recorder, a large professional unit with 16-inch tape reels. The machine weighed more than 50 pounds.

Not only was Marilyn on time, she was friendly and cooperative and gave us an unforgettable interview. When it was over, she asked if she could add something and, of course, we said yes. She ad-libbed a touching and heartwarming tribute to the servicemen and women, thanking them for listening and wishing them the very best of luck.

She was beautiful, bright and charming. She was the Marilyn we'll always remember.

TONY DiMARCO ◆ LOS ANGELES, CA

Tony DiMarco, left, and his colleague Dave Ketchum were impressed by Marilyn Monroe's professionalism and sincerity when they interviewed her for their Army radio show in 1952.

FUN FACTS

BORN NORMA JEANE MORTENSON, Marilyn Monroe didn't take her stage name until 1946—and the first time someone asked her for her autograph, she had to check how to spell "Marilyn." Many mistakenly believed her to be as dim as her characters. In fact, her collection of 400-plus books included works on Abraham Lincoln, fiction by Ernest Hemingway and Theodore Dreiser, and classics by John Milton and Walt Whitman.

“ Marilyn Monroe was always the number one choice of the GIs. ”

Poetic License

For the great Robert Frost, the best anthology of poetry was the one not written.

DAVID NEAL KELLER ◆ DUBLIN, OH

As a member of the administrative staff at Ohio University in Athens, Ohio, I had the pleasant assignment of escorting the dean of American poetry, Robert Frost, around the campus during his two-day visit there in the spring of 1960. This involved accompanying him while he visited literature classes, read his poems at a convocation, and—the thing he said he liked best—strolled the grounds, talking with the students.

"I learn so much from the things they tell me," he said.

Students were enchanted by their encounters with the 85-year-old and four-time Pulitzer Prize winner, who in 1961 would become the first poet to take part in a presidential inauguration ceremony.

His responses to the students seemed so natural yet so profound that I couldn't determine whether they were spontaneous or thought out in advance.

David Keller spent two memorable days with the celebrated poet in 1960.

His most memorable remark obviously was preplanned, though I have never encountered it in print. He said, "It's only having been contrasted that bad and good so long have lasted."

One of the few times we were alone, I mentioned in passing that I wrote part time and hoped to make it a career. I tried to drop the subject quickly so it wouldn't seem that I was seeking his advice. But his reaction was as abrupt as it was startling.

"Well, whatever you do," he said gruffly, "don't write an anthology." He went on to deride the concept of anthologies, including those around his own poetry. All they amount to are collections of works "accompanied by the collectors' interpretations of meanings the authors never intended."

Then a devilish twinkle glowed in his eyes. "I don't ordinarily make such an admission on a college campus because I'm certain you have professors here who do anthologies." He added conspiratorially, "I'll expect you to say nothing about it until I'm dead and gone."

Later I realized he must have been testing me, but I never was sure. I played it safe, in any case, never putting it in writing until now, though Robert Frost died in 1963.

I also have never given the slightest thought to doing an anthology.

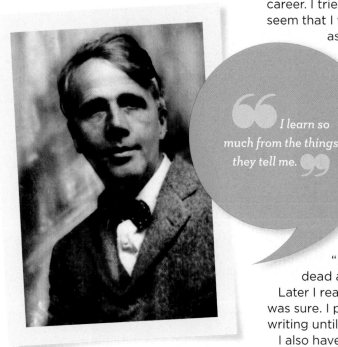

I learn so much from the things they tell me.

Robert Frost

In Mexico with Flynn

Her aunt's fleeting relationship with Errol Flynn was purely platonic.

DIANE DE ANDA ◆ PLAYA DEL REY, CA

Contrary to all the gossip and his legendary reputation, Errol Flynn could be a gentleman. So says my aunt Maria Monay, who befriended him for a short time when her career collided with his in Mexico.

The studio filming *The Sun Also Rises* was throwing a birthday party for Tyrone Power, one of the stars of the movie. Maria was working in Mexico as a model at the time and was invited to attend. She lined up with the well-wishers to offer birthday greetings to the guest of honor. While all the women gushed over the famously handsome Power and gave him kisses, Maria knew him as only a screen figure, so she simply shook his hand.

Maria Monay spent time with movie star Errol Flynn while modeling in Mexico.

Audrey Hepburn and husband Mel Ferrer sat on a sofa, surrounded by a parade of single beauties. My aunt was in a corner talking to producer Darryl Zanuck and another man when Ava Gardner made a grand entrance with her entourage.

As Maria worked her way to the buffet table, she found herself standing next to Errol Flynn. He was struggling with a square of Jell-O that eventually jiggled off his plate and onto the floor. Undeterred, he plucked the square from where it had landed and put it on his plate.

"Uh-uh," Maria said, shaking her head. He smiled as she removed the sullied piece and shuffled a clean square onto his plate.

Their acquaintance might have ended there had it not been for her friend Rosa, who was Flynn's local caretaker. When he was struck by a bout of Montezuma's revenge, Flynn called Rosa for her folk cure.

Rosa asked my aunt to accompany her to his hotel room, where they found him in bed, covered with blankets. He made an impish joke about their joining him, but the women just laughed, knowing that it wasn't a true proposition.

So began a friendship for the next few weeks in Mexico. Maria and Errol went to lunch, dinner and nightclubs together and shared some quiet conversations.

She told me that she was not smitten with him as so many other women were, partly because she was nursing a broken heart from a recent break-up. And he was in the early stages of a relationship back in the States.

So they just enjoyed each other's company, my Aunt Maria and Errol Flynn, the gentleman.

The Night Debbie Reynolds Was My Dad's Girlfriend

Her dad suddenly was part of the show. **LOU ANN GURNEY** ♦ KEAAU, HI

On a family trip to Lake Tahoe in 1975, my dad tried to get tickets to see Sammy Davis Jr., but that event was sold out. He came back with tickets for the Debbie Reynolds dinner show instead. I wasn't expecting much, to be honest. Debbie definitely did not have Sammy's hip-cool factor.

My dad, always outgoing and gregarious, was dressed in bright yellow slacks and jacket with white patent leather shoes. He was sporting his signature goatee, too. He tipped the maître d' and we got a front row table.

No sooner had the show started than Debbie sashayed off the stage, into the audience

The Gurneys, Lou Ann, Evadale and Wayne (above), relax in their Lake Tahoe hotel room before going to Debbie Reynolds' dinner show in 1975. Note that Wayne wears his snazzy white patent shoes. Wayne Gurney (left) shows off his impressive goatee.

and straight up to my father, Wayne. She sat flirtatiously in his lap and talked to him while stroking his goatee. After learning my mother's name, Evadale, Debbie had the entire audience shout, "Hi Wayne! How's Little Eva?" That became the catchphrase of the evening.

She continued to mention my father at various points throughout her show. For example, when a cast member who was a body builder flexed his muscles, Debbie quipped, "Wayne taught him how to do that." Then she'd signal for the catchphrase and the audience would shout, "Hi Wayne! How's Little Eva?"

Debbie's show was fantastic that night—with singing, dancing, a chorus line, gorgeous costumes, humor. Best of all, she gave my father a taste of the limelight, a place he loved to be.

After the show, numerous people in the casino greeted Dad with the catchphrase—even hours later, as we were walking into a different casino.

I'm sure Sammy Davis Jr.'s performance was great, but I can't imagine that he would have perched on Dad's lap and made him a part of his act. Debbie Reynolds created a treasured memory for us.

Forever after, we called Debbie Reynolds "Dad's girlfriend."

SIGHTS FOR SORE EYES

STARTING IN THE SECOND GRADE in 1968, I had to go into Manhattan every six months to have my eyes examined by a doctor at Lexington Avenue and 39th Street. My appointment was usually around 10:30 a.m.

Afterward, my mother and I would walk to the ticket office underneath the Park Avenue Viaduct to get free passes to various TV tapings that day.

We went to lots of shows, but the few I remember were the original *Jeopardy!* with Art Fleming; *Concentration* with Jack Narz; and *To Tell The Truth*, after which I got autographs from Kitty Carlisle, Peggy Cass, Durward Kirby and Bill Cullen, who was himself a host of numerous game shows.

Sometimes Lillian Miller, known as Miss Miller or Mrs. Miller, was in the audience. She later became famous for her regular attendance at tapings of *The Tonight Show*, *The Carol Burnett Show* and *The Merv Griffin Show*.

RICHARD MICHAEL TUSUSIAN ◆ BAYSIDE, NY

Master of Ceremonies Bud Collyer (rear) hosted *To Tell The Truth* on CBS, which Richard got to see in person as a child. Panelists shown in the photo are (from left) Polly Bergen, Ralph Bellamy, Kitty Carlisle and Hy Gardner.

SIGN OF THE TIMES

HUNDREDS SCRAMBLED to get Dick Clark's autograph when he came to McGuire Air Force Base in New Jersey on Armed Forces Day 1957, recalls Robert Lonstad of Colona, Illinois. An airman second class, 18-year-old Robert took a break from airplane maintenance to see the show. "I have to say Dick Clark aged very well. Years later, he looked the same as he does in this picture."

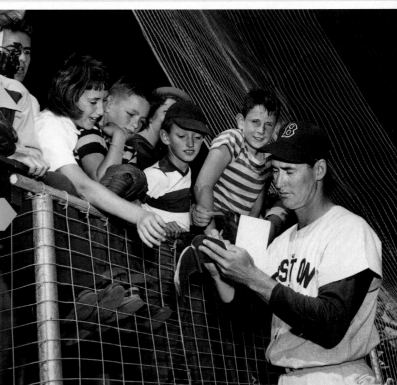

LEGEND MAKES HIS MARK

BOSTON RED SOX outfielder Ted Williams delighted young and old with his batting prowess in 19 seasons between 1939 and 1960. He holds the record for highest career on-base percentage. Here he signs autographs for eager young fans.

INSTANT AMERICAN DREAM

JOYCE RICHARDS CASE, right, won a trip to Las Vegas, Nevada, on the Hollywood game show *Temptation*— and met singer Connie Francis after a show at the Sahara hotel. Joyce now resides in New Iberia, Louisiana.

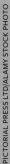

When Mom and I found out that Bette Davis' TV show The Dark Secret of Harvest Home *(1978) was filming in Kingsville, Ohio, we had to go. Sadly, we saw only her trailer that day.*

KATHLEEN McDONALD ◆ ERIE, PA

HAPPY HOLIDAYS

There's certainly no place like home for the holidays, and these photos and stories serve as warm reminders of precious times with family and friends.

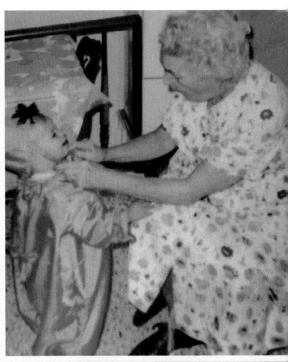

CHAPTER 10

Let the Good Times Roll!

Four decades after she fell for Mardi Gras on the silver screen, she got to experience it live. **CAROL ANNE LAKE** ◆ PORT CLINTON, OH

The Mardi Gras bug bit me back in 1959 when I was only 9—thanks to the movie *Mardi Gras* starring Pat Boone and Christine Carère. Christine played the queen of the Mardi Gras parade, who wore a ball gown fit for a princess and threw strands of beads to the crowd. I decided then and there that someday I'd come home with my own treasure trove of beads.

I finally made my Mardi Gras dreams come true in 2000. Having waited 41 years, I wanted the full experience. So my husband, Jim, and I took Amtrak's City of New Orleans train (decked out in gold, green and purple) from Chicago, Illinois, to The Big Easy in Louisiana. Once in New Orleans, I was thrilled to learn of a parade that very night! Even with beads flying everywhere, my first catch was a plastic cup—which now occupies a spot of honor on my bookshelf.

Throughout all the exquisite dining, shopping and sightseeing that followed, it was still all about the parades for me. With every procession that worked its way through the French Quarter, I threw my hands in the air, yelling: "Throw me some beads, mister!"

Finally I couldn't pile any more strands around my neck, so I focused on the high school bands and beautiful floats. So much effort went into entertaining visitors.

Jim and I were lucky enough to attend the Endymion Extravaganza, a formal ball held at the Superdome. (Endymion is one of Mardi Gras' "super krewes.")

> *The magic of Mardi Gras endures the passage of time.*

The Endymion parade made several rounds within the Superdome, with krewe members tossing out beads, doubloons, cups, stuffed animals and moon pies. This party (which included the rock band Chicago) went on into the wee hours of the morning, when a mile-long line of taxis waited to take partygoers back to their hotels.

But I still had one more Mardi Gras experience I needed to fulfill—to throw beads myself. So the next year I joined the Mystic Krewe of Barkus on behalf of my dog, Gypsy. In 2005, she had the honor of walking in the Barkus parade. I held her leash and threw strands of beads that featured bones and a medallion that said "Wassup Dog!" The crowd loved them.

The magic of Mardi Gras endures the passage of time. And it was just like in the movies, only better.

Carol Anne models a headdress at Mardi Gras World, a New Orleans attraction that lets visitors try on costumes.

AS DESCENDANTS of a long line of New Orleanians, Ron and Linda Conaway wanted to make sure their children took part in Mardi Gras fun. In 1972, the Conaway kids dressed as clowns, wearing pompom-decorated costumes made by Ron's mother, Mathilda Meyers Conaway. Clockwise from top left, the jesters are Ron Jr., 8, Mark, 6, Darrin, 2, and Michael, 4.

READY FOR THE BANQUET

CLEARLY TRESSED TO IMPRESS, 15-year-old Barbara Bierbrodt, now of Southaven, Mississippi, accessorized her beehive with fresh daisies. The occasion? An annual Valentine's Day banquet in the early 1960s at her church, in the Memphis, Tennessee, area. Her mom, Frances South, made the gown of red dotted swiss. "I remember feeling so special that night, like a princess," Barbara says.

EASTER SUNDAY BEST

MARTIN LEE KLUG AND BIG BROTHER RICHARD, posing here with their father, Leo Klug, always looked forward to Easter in the 1950s. They would wear their new outfits to church, then they'd get baskets before going to their grandparents' in Baltimore, Maryland, for Easter dinner. Martin now resides in Swanton, Maryland.

SITTIN' PRETTY

"THIS IS MY MOM, Alice Hurst, with my brother Tom in 1951 in California," says Kathy Gastellu of Buckeye, Arizona. "Mom is still looking cover-girl beautiful today."

EGGS-CELLENT JOB

JUST BEFORE EASTER in 1959, Peggy Oels, 4, now of Glendale, Arizona, and her sister Kathy, 7, look up briefly from their egg-dyeing duties at their home in Tucson, Arizona.

Easter Hat for a Queen

In 1963, I entered a third-grade Easter pageant at Swanson Elementary in Omaha, Nebraska. Contestants had to make Easter hats at home, and judges picked a winner based on originality. For my hat, Mom and I took a small lampshade, added two long strips of heavy cardboard, and covered the whole creation with cotton balls. The result was a big rabbit head!

Later, at the contest, all the other girls wore straw hats with plastic flowers glued on, while I donned my rabbit head. Walking onstage to the tune of "Easter Parade," each girl was greeted with applause; I was greeted with laughter. But in the end, the joke was on them: The judges awarded me the title of Easter Queen for having the most original hat!

DEBRA MASTERA ◆ LINCOLN, NE

....

Bunny Surprise

I grew up in Kansas City, Missouri, the eldest of five children. The Great Depression was in full swing in 1934, and I was 5 years old. For weeks, all I could think about was the Easter bunny. When Easter Sunday finally arrived, I rushed to see what the bunny had brought. I was stunned to see eggs on the living-room floor, tracing a straight line from the center of the room to the front door. "Someone must have scared the bunny, and he dropped the eggs as he ran for the door," my daddy explained.

> *For weeks, all I could think about was the Easter bunny.*

This was one of many tales he told us as we grew up. His father died before he was born, and his mother never remarried. Daddy was an only child. He was reliving his childhood as he wished it would have been—and having a great time.

FRAN MILLION ◆ FREMONT, NE

"I TREASURE THIS PICTURE of me (left) with my cousins Kathleen, Sandy, Cathy, Pam and Carol in our Easter finery in El Monte, California, in 1957," says Gail Perry of Phelan, California. "I still have that shawl and bonnet my Granny Catherine made for me."

PEDALING IN THE PARADE

JANE WHITT GREW UP in White Lake, a village in northern Wisconsin, and she fondly recalls the Fourth of July parades every year, as seen in these photos from 1970. "I remember how exciting it was to decorate my bike with streamers, flags and noisemakers," says Jane, now of Stevens Point, Wisconsin. "Seemed as if every kid in town was riding, pushing or pulling a red, white and blue bike, wagon or stroller. The bands, the floats and so many veterans—it was the first time most of us knew what it meant to feel patriotic."

"MY MOTHER, Anne Krisak, was 10 when she posed in 1937 as the Statue of Liberty for her school in Detroit, Michigan," says Renee Gensor of Washington Township, Michigan. "She and my father taught us that the statue stood for freedom and hope—as it had for their parents, who all emigrated from Slovakia."

TRICK OR TREAT

Most likely, the practice of trick-or-treating, originally called guising, started in Britain during the Middle Ages, when children and the poor dressed up during All Hallows' Day and went door-to-door asking for food and money in exchange for a song or prayer for the dead.

The first reference to "trick or treat" appears in a 1927 *Lethbridge* (Alberta) *Herald*. The taunt, it says, was used by youthful revelers demanding treats in lieu of tricks played if they were refused.

....

2,324
Weight in pounds of the record-setting world's largest pumpkin. The enormous squash was grown in Switzerland in 2014.

....

$308.5
In millions, box office revenue for the *Halloween* franchise.

....

35
In millions, the number of pounds of candy corn produced each year.

Karen dressed as Cinderella; her little brother, Evart, was a ghost; and her sister, Janice, was Little Red Riding Hood.

> *All along the way, he dragged his paper trick-or-treat bag through every puddle.*

Girls, Share with Your Brother

A wet Halloween provided an unwelcomed opportunity for a sibling candy exchange.

KAREN WITHERS ◆ MILLINGTON, MI

It was so cold and rainy the Halloween of 1965 that we had to wear coats. What I remember most about it, though, was that it was my brother Evart's worst Halloween ever. He was short and had to run to keep up. All along the way, he dragged his paper trick-or-treat bag through every puddle. By the time we got home, there wasn't a single piece of candy left in his bag. He was in tears. So were my sister and I when Mom made us share our candy with him.

HALLOWEEN IS COMING

IN ALLENTOWN, PENNSYLVANIA, where Phyllis Guth and her husband, Paul, grew up, trick-or-treating started in mid-October. Phyllis and her girlfriends often entertained neighbors with renditions of "Oh My Darling, Clementine" and "You Are My Sunshine."

Phyllis, now of neighboring Whitehall, says they would finish with a recitation: "Halloween is coming and the goose is getting fat. Will you please put a penny in the old man's hat?" Adds Phyllis, "Most people gave us a nickel, dime or occasionally a quarter—that was a lot in the 1940s."

ONE-OF-A-KIND COSTUMES

CAROLYN HEEP'S MOM, Opal Phillips, was a talented seamstress who sewed all the clothes for her daughter and granddaughters in Del Rio, Texas. In 1978 she made Halloween costumes for Carolyn's daughters Debbie, near right, and Sandy, using her own patterns. The girls looked forward to wearing the costumes their grandmother made.

HAIR-RAISING HALLOWEEN

SALLY OLSON from Harbor Springs, Michigan, shared this photo of her younger siblings Peter and Laura tugging at Laura's yarn braids while they celebrate Halloween 1964 in their uncle Don Brandt's den in Dearborn Heights, Michigan.

Kimberly, Gran's great-great-granddaughter, makes a supercute Halloween clown in 1993.

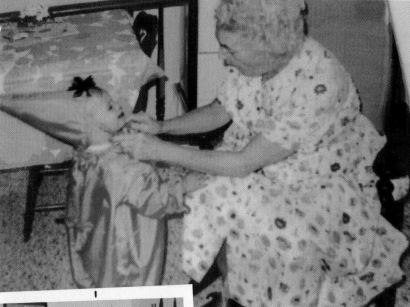

Above, Gran ties the clown hat under great-granddaughter Kristine's chin. At left, Kristine gives her brother, Jim, a turn in the cheery clown costume in 1972.

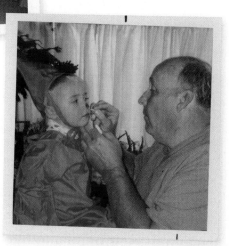

In 2002, Jim, Gran's oldest grandson, applies makeup just so on his granddaughter Brooke's nose.

Our Cast of Clowns

Our oldest daughter was excited in October 1969 to go trick-or-treating with her family and friends. She was 1½ years old, and her great-grandmother wanted to make her a costume. What fun!

Gran, as we called her, had some shiny fabric that she thought would be perfect to use to make a clown outfit for her first great-granddaughter, Kristine. My husband, Jim, was Gran's oldest grandson.

The costume included black pompoms made from yarn and a hat that fit perfectly.

As our family grew, both our son, Jim Jr., and youngest daughter, Jacquelyn, wore the costume, as well as all eight of our grandchildren.

Today, Jacquelyn keeps the costume at her home, well preserved and looking brand-new. Jim and I look forward to a time when our first great-grandchild will wear it.

Our entire family feels blessed to have this memory of Gran and her handiwork as part of our family history.

EILEEN MATTISON ◆ HACKETTSTOWN, NJ

Disappearing Heads

One Halloween night in Floral, Arkansas, in the late 1950s, my cousin Teresa and I got together to go trick-or-treating. We were about 9 or 10, and my older sister, Jeanette, was taking us. In all honesty, Jeanette probably didn't want the job of driving us kids around, but she got stuck with it.

On that night, my sister pulled to the side of the road at the first house. Had she pulled into the driveway, everything would have been all right. We would have seen how to get to the front door.

Instead we had to run across the yard to get to the house, and it was pretty dark outside. So we bounded out of her car with our brown paper bags in hand. My sister said she watched our little heads bobbing up and down as we trotted toward the house. Then suddenly, we completely disappeared.

As for Teresa and me, we got a big shock as we went flying downward into a huge freshly dug hole in the neighbor's front yard. To this day, I still don't know why that hole happened there. I do know it was a wonder we didn't end up with some sort of injury. Somehow, we composed ourselves enough to climb out of the hole and get to the porch to trick-or-treat without complaining.

Meanwhile, back at the car, my sister was rolling with laughter. When Teresa and I returned to the car with our paper bags, Jeanette acted out the sight she'd seen, holding up fingers to represent the two of us and then clenching her fist to show how our heads vanished in the darkness.

Back then, we weren't quite as cheerful as Jeanette was about the whole thing, but now Teresa and I still laugh whenever the incident comes up. Although we recovered and got our treat—homemade popcorn balls—it was a pretty funny, although unintended, trick.

ANGELINE STONER ◆ FLORAL, AR

LIGHTING UP THE NIGHT

WHEN YOUR DAD is a service technician for IBM, it stands to reason that all those electronics could be used to make a blinking robot costume for Halloween. Sure enough, Peggy Oels of Glendale, Arizona, wore the uncomfortable suit that her dad and mom made in 1963. "I couldn't sit down," Peggy says. "And the battery pack for the lights whacked me on top of my head." She fooled the neighbors, though. They thought for sure the robot coming to the door had to be a boy.

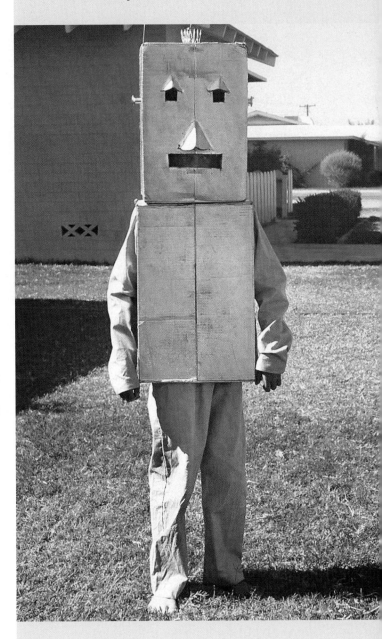

Dishing Up for the Camera

When Mom's best dishes didn't quite suffice for an important shoot, a photographer made a kind gesture. **JUDY SIKORSKI** ◆ ROSSFORD, OH

Ladies Home Journal selected our family for its "How America Lives" feature in 1948. The reporter and photographer arrived at the end of May and followed all of us (Mom, Dad, my brother, my sister and me) for a week, recording our every move. Everyone was pretty excited about it, especially in our town of 6,000, where things like this just didn't happen.

Since the article would be published in late October, we had to pretend it was already autumn. The reporter asked our mom to cook and serve a complete Thanksgiving meal. She told Mom to "go all out" and use her best holiday dishes for the feast.

Mom's face fell. She didn't want to admit that our best dishes weren't exactly the best, let alone suitable for a national magazine. While the reporter continued with her interview, the photographer quietly excused himself and slipped away for over an hour. When he came back, he had a large box, which he placed on the floor, telling Mom to open it.

Her face lit up as if it was Christmas. Inside was a very beautiful set of dishes, a service for 12 trimmed in gold, made by the Homer Laughlin China Co. There was even a soup tureen, something we kids had never seen before. Mom was near tears as she lovingly handled each piece.

When it came time to serve dinner, Mom walked slowly from the kitchen with the lovely new platter, which contained a small "turkey" (in reality, it was a large chicken).

Mom cherished those dishes and made sure they never saw the light of day unless it was a major event, though they were a must every Thanksgiving.

I carry on the tradition, using the dishes for our Thanksgiving feast. But I serve a real turkey, and I serve it on the real Thanksgiving Day.

Judy's mother, Mary Schultz, was delighted to serve dinner on her new dishes, courtesy of a thoughtful *Ladies Home Journal* photographer.

> " *Mom was near tears as she lovingly handled each piece.* "

IN 1917 MY FATHER, Pvt. William A. Gallagher, served in the 16th Calvary, Troop F, during World War I. The Thanksgiving menu at Fort Brown, Brownsville, Texas, where he was stationed, included oyster dressing, succotash and pie.

Almost four decades later in 1955, I was a private first class at Fort Knox, Kentucky, when specialties on the Thanksgiving menu included shrimp cocktail, candied sweet potatoes and pumpkin pie.

CARL GALLAGHER ◆ HASLETT, MI

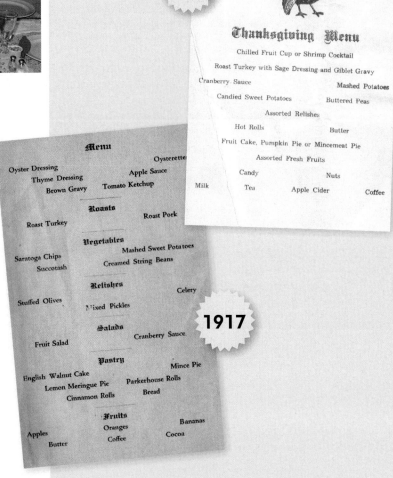

1955

Thanksgiving Menu

Chilled Fruit Cup or Shrimp Cocktail

Roast Turkey with Sage Dressing and Giblet Gravy

Cranberry Sauce   Mashed Potatoes

Candied Sweet Potatoes   Buttered Peas

Assorted Relishes

Hot Rolls   Butter

Fruit Cake, Pumpkin Pie or Mincemeat Pie

Assorted Fresh Fruits

Candy   Nuts

Milk   Tea   Apple Cider   Coffee

1917

Menu

Oyster Dressing   Oysterettes
Thyme Dressing   Apple Sauce
Brown Gravy   Tomato Ketchup

Roasts
Roast Turkey   Roast Pork

Vegetables
Saratoga Chips   Mashed Sweet Potatoes
Succotash   Creamed String Beans

Relishes
Stuffed Olives   Celery
Mixed Pickles

Salads
Fruit Salad   Cranberry Sauce

Pastry
English Walnut Cake   Mince Pie
Lemon Meringue Pie   Parkerhouse Rolls
Cinnamon Rolls   Bread

Fruits
Apples   Oranges   Bananas
Butter   Coffee   Cocoa

Thanksgiving Shakers

We gathered at the table just before eating in Elmira, New York, in 1959. I'm in the red shirt between my grandmother and my mother, Jean. Next to her are my aunt Dot O'Herron and my siblings Joy, Paul (who's also pictured in the bottom photo in 1954), Carol, and Steve, who shields his eyes from the camera's flash. Flanking the cornucopia centerpiece are the turkey salt and pepper shakers that never missed a Thanksgiving.

When my widowed father sold the house 33 years later, I looked for those shakers, but they were so chipped and worn that I decided not to take them. Now I wish I had!

TOM HUONKER ◆ ROCHESTER, NY

Cracking Good Fun

You could always expect two things from Uncle Willie: full volume and high energy. Every visit was punctuated by his booming voice and irrepressible spirit. He was a table-pounder, a shouter and sharer, a man with a flair for the dramatic. No dinner with him was ever boring. I looked forward to him coming over every holiday.

My mother's turkey platter was a point of pride for her. She displayed it on top of our cabinet above the kitchen table when it wasn't in use. One summer day, my Uncle Willie sat at the kitchen table, gesturing and shouting as he always did, and when he came to a big point he wanted to make—*BAM!*—he thumped the table with his fist.

CRASH! The turkey platter came clattering down from its perch and landed right in front of Uncle Willie. The platter now had a hairline crack running from rim to rim. There was a brief beat of silence, and then we all started to chuckle. Willie apologized, but no one was too angry. After all, it had truly been an accident, and maybe the turkey platter wasn't ruined after all.

Uncle Willie has been gone for more than 35 years now, but we still use the turkey platter every year, crack and all. With its imperfections, the platter is even more special to our family— because in a way, it brings Willie back to us, still making his mark on every holiday dinner.

MARLIES PALKA ◆ WYNANTSKILL, NY

> *These salt and pepper shakers have graced our Thanksgiving table since the 1950s. Our grandchildren love to see them every year.*

ELLEN SCOTT ◆ NAPLES, FL

SERVICE WITH A GOBBLE

"MY MOTHER had this platter when she got married in 1949," says Maggie Tullie of Micco, Florida. "My father was in the service so it has been in Germany, France, Alaska, Kentucky, Nevada and Florida. I won't let anyone else touch it; that is how precious it is to me."

Jeannine has created a unique family heirloom by embroidering the doodles of guests each Thanksgiving. A young guest (below) makes her mark to be preserved by Jeannine's artistry.

Stitched in Time

An accident starts a beloved tradition for years to come. **JEANNINE MEINEN** ◆ BELLEVILLE, IL

In 1989, after Thanksgiving dinner, one of my grandchildren drew something on the tablecloth. It was so good that I wanted to keep it, and I came up with the idea to embroider it. Then I asked everyone to sign the tablecloth for me to embroider as a keepsake.

This has now become our family tradition. We have more than 35 people at our Thanksgiving dinners, which are held at my son's lake house.

I write down the names of everyone who was at dinner, take the cloth home, and cross the names off as I embroider them, so I don't miss anyone. Then I wash and iron it for the next year.

We have some real art on this cloth, as well as stick people, children's hand tracings, hearts, sayings, names and dates. We even have a scribbling from a baby. I stitch it all.

Overnight Sensation

Birthdays and Christmas in the same week created many memories. **JAMES FREY** ◆ OSHKOSH, WI

1962

M y mother's birthday was on Christmas Eve, mine was two days after Christmas, and my dad's was two days after mine. With our three birthdays and Christmas all within six days, Christmastime meant a full week of celebrations.

When I went to bed on Christmas Eve anticipating Santa's visit, there was no evidence of Christmas in our house. But after I fell asleep, my mother and dad spent hours setting up everything—toys and decorations—just to surprise me!

On Christmas morning when I got up, a fully decorated Christmas tree stood on a large elevated platform with electric trains running through a miniature village. The village was realistically scaled and included cotton cut to fit between the tracks to replicate snow. The festive living room was filled with piles of toys and presents amid the furniture. It was an amazing sight.

> 66 *When I went to bed on Christmas Eve anticipating Santa's visit, there was no evidence of Christmas in our house.* 99

THIS COLORFUL KARO AD ran as a full page, while ad copy on one-third of the adjacent page (not shown) contained a basic candy recipe—Karo, margarine, vanilla and confectioners' sugar— and directions for making all the treats on display. The ad touts Karo as "a wholesome kind of sweetness" because it adds "dextrose—a sugar that needs no digestion!"

On his second birthday, two days after Christmas 1942, James Frey shows how to get more cake.

Christmas Directing Debut

A modest production earns applause.

RUTH McNEILL ◆ CORVALLIS, OR

Whether I was writing or directing them, Christmas plays were a highlight of my childhood. I was 8 in 1957 when I came up with the idea for a revised nativity story. The three kings would get together in their old age to recall the long trip they made to Bethlehem in their youth. I was mostly in charge but got a lot of help and support from my mother.

The cast members and I painted the palace scenery on brown paper in our basement while Mother supervised. We held rehearsals in our dining room, and I suggested what the actors should say.

The morning of the performance, Mother hung the scenery across the swinging door between the dining room and the kitchen. Dad pushed the heavy dining room table on its casters into the living room. My sister and I collected every chair in the house and set them up in rows facing the palace and the adjacent alcove, where most of the action would take place.

The three old kings (above left) kibitzed about the terrible roads, the weather and uncooperative camels on the way to Bethlehem. Above, the actors came early and dressed in their costumes made from leftover fabric.

Throughout the three scenes of the play, children from the neighborhood paraded through our dining room dressed in robes, rags, shawls and make-do crowns or halos. For that short time, they became kings, shepherds, angels and, of course, Mary and Joseph. One little angel had a stain on her robe, but nobody seemed to care; after all, she was only 3.

At the end of the play, the cast stood and bowed in jagged unison. I loved the applause; still, I had to ask Mother about the spot on the angel's robe. She told me, "The poor thing was so anxious about her role that she threw up, so I cleaned her up as best I could."

Santa Brought Him a Chevy

He was already well-acquainted with his gift. **BRIAN DANKERT** • SANFORD, MI

After graduating from Arthur Hill High School in Saginaw, Michigan, in 1963, I started working at Baywood Party Store. The only mode of transportation I had was a Triumph motorcycle, which I'd bought when I graduated. That was not the best way to get around in Michigan with winter coming.

My sister Gail had a 1954 Chevy that she'd bought from our parents while she was interning in Detroit. She offered to sell it back to Mom and Dad because she was getting married and didn't need it anymore. That way I would have something to drive.

I drove it off and on, any time it snowed. My brother Ron would use the car, too, whenever he was home from college. He was rough on it. Once he power shifted into second gear—shifting without easing up on the accelerator—and broke the linkage and column rod. He said it looked like a bomb site. Ron took the poor Chevy over to the garage where he used to work and, with his buddies, fixed everything before anyone saw the damage.

Meanwhile, little did I know that the family had decided to give me the car for Christmas that year. I came downstairs on Christmas morning, looked out the window, and saw my present in the driveway. My dad and brother-in-law had put a small tree on the Chevy. They told me they couldn't put the car under the Christmas tree so they put the tree on top of the car.

I really enjoyed that Christmas present all winter while the snow was blowing. It sure was warmer than the motorcycle.

Chevy Christmas! Brian's dad and brother-in-law put a Charlie Brown-like tree on the old sedan so Brian would know the car was his Christmas present.

I looked out and saw my present in the driveway.

Brite with Possibilities

I have been collecting vintage Christmas tree ornaments for 30 years, starting with the Shiny Brite bulbs I remembered from my childhood. I would often find them at flea markets for $1 a box.

Through the years, I have watched the prices of these machine-blown glass ornaments skyrocket. Selling them on eBay has been lucrative, as well as enjoyable, for me.

Several vintage ornaments made in Germany are part of my collection. These brightly colored ornaments are very thin glass and terribly fragile.

I also have many Shiny Brites in their original boxes, which are as hard to find as the ornaments themselves. Some of the WWII-era ornaments are "unsilvered," decorated with paint or small white mica crystals on the outside but no shiny coating inside.

Ornaments with paper caps are easy to date. They were made during WWII when metal could not be used.

I love collecting ornaments; it is a great hobby. I enjoy going to flea markets, and I never know what rarity I will come across.

WILLIAM OGDEN ◆ WOOSTER, OH

American-made Shiny Brite ornaments were machine-blown and hand-decorated.

FROM SHINY TO BRIGHT

EARLY CHRISTMAS TREE decorations in America were often handmade, as store-bought glass or paper imports from Europe were expensive.

UNTIL THE MID-1920s, most imported blown-glass ornaments in the U.S. came from Germany.

WHEN WAR IN EUROPE threatened ornament supplies to the U.S. in the late 1930s, Max Eckardt, a German immigrant and ornament importer, persuaded Corning Glass Works of New York to modify its lightbulb-making machines and start producing glass ornaments.

CORNING SHIPPED its first mass-produced glass ornaments in December 1939 to Woolworth stores. They sold for 2 to 10 cents each.

MATERIAL SHORTAGES during WWII forced design changes. Pastel-colored stripes on clear balls replaced shiny silvering and lacquer, and cardboard caps replaced metal ones.

Source: Bob Richter, A Very Vintage Christmas, 2016

PRESENTS FOR THOSE ABSENT

IN 1944 Carol Hanson Stirling, 2, of Hammond, Indiana, sits near photos of a family friend and her brothers Paul (bottom right) and Virgil (not shown), who were serving in WWII. "We kept their gifts until they returned home," she says.

MIRACLE IN NEWARK?

LOOKING LIKE NATALIE WOOD in *Miracle on 34th Street,* 4-year-old Gertrude Bumiller, now of Keansburg, New Jersey, talks to Santa Claus at a Macy's store in Newark around 1948. The classic movie, released in 1947, also involves a Macy's Santa, but at the store's flagship location in New York City.

PLAYING DOCTOR

ON CHRISTMAS MORNING in 1961, Jean Bordt of Lexington, Kentucky, received a Chatty Cathy doll, while her brother Jimmy got a doctor kit. Chatty Cathy was Jimmy's first patient.

"I LEAVE THESE SPECIAL Christmas collectibles out all year," says Ronda Garnett of West Des Moines, Iowa. "Most belonged to my grandmother Elaine Six, who passed away in 1970 at the age of 54. We called her Grandma Lane. She worked at the dime store in downtown Des Moines, and I'm sure that she accumulated them at after-holiday sales. It makes me happy to see them every day."

HOLIDAY PUPS

BOBBIE DAVENPORT (wearing headband) of Huntsville, Alabama, and her twin sister, Becky, got their furry friends in 1964. "We had gone two long, sad months without a dog in our house. We came home and found these adorable puppies, Bebe (left) and Buffy, waiting for us," Bobbie writes.

SADDLE UP!

NEW YORKER MARY SULLIVAN proudly poses in the authentic Dale Evans outfit she received on Christmas morning 1951. "I loved my outfit and wore it constantly for two years," says Mary. "Unfortunately, Dad said no to Buttermilk (Dale's horse) because there wasn't room for a barn in our backyard." Mary adds that she was—in her imaginary world—a valued member of the Dale Evans posse.

"My grandpa Edward Brown would dress up as Santa and go around our neighborhood in Ottawa, Illinois, handing out candy to kids. This photo must have been taken in the late 1940s, and ran in the local paper shortly after Grandpa died. The caption called him 'a big man with a heart to match.'"

DAVID BROWN ◆ MODESTO, CA